SURVIVING YOUR FIRST YEAR OF COLLEGE

SURVIVING YOUR FIRST YEAR OF COLLEGE

Michael A. Kipp
+ Sandy Kipp

bare
foot
MINISTRIES®
KANSAS CITY, MISSOURI

Copyright 2012 by Barefoot Ministries®

ISBN 978-0-8341-5063-8

Printed in the United States of America

Editor: Audra C. Marvin
Cover Design: J.R. Caines
Interior Design: Sharon Page and J.R. Caines

Library of Congress Cataloging-in-Publication Data: 2011939319

10 9 8 7 6 5 4 3 2 1

CONTENTS

Car or Bike?
Home
Finding a Church
Athletics
Avoiding Common Pitfalls
Good Luck

INTRODUCTION

I attended a different university or college each of my first four years after high school. Crazy, eh? I did not plan to do that; it just sort of happened.

I had always planned to attend college. During my junior year of high school, I sent out applications to schools I thought I would like to attend in my home state. I had *no* idea what I was actually interested in doing or studying. At the time, I was only interested in being close to the beach. That did not lend itself to making a wise decision and set up my transition to another school almost from the beginning.

Years later, I now find myself teaching at a university. In my role as professor, I have the distinct privilege of interacting with prospective students as well as current college students. Something I am more and more convinced of is the considerable importance of choosing the *right* school. And the right school does not only mean a desirable location. In fact, the location can quickly become a secondary issue when compared to other important matters. Although in reality some students might love the beach, the very best place for them to go to college might not be near an ocean since it could present itself as a large distraction from the primary task at hand—studying. However, with the right expectations and personal discipline, there is no reason why you cannot have the beach and study too.

My experience at four different schools actually turned out pretty well, but I would not recommend anyone setting out to do what I did. I think choosing the right institution and staying there for your entire college career is the more desirable alternative. The relationships formed over time with not only peers but faculty and staff are of immeasurable value. While a person learns a great deal in the classroom during college, it is the lifelong relationships formed during your twenties (and after) that will sustain you through your journey in this life. Can you imagine the depth those relationships would be able to reach over the years rather than just several months? If I could change what I did, I would find the right school the first time and stay there. That's my first piece of advice to you.

Getting advice from someone who's already experienced something can be helpful. That is part of the reason I have written this book. But my experience is limited, so I have also attempted to leverage that by including throughout this book advice from other students, administrators, and faculty that will help frame the things I write here. Of course, I encourage you to test all that is included here by bouncing it off your friends and relatives. They know you and will be better able to advise you on specific issues than any book ever could.

If you are one of the fortunate ones who is able to choose a good college the first time and then stay there, this does not automatically mean you are limiting your experiences. There are numerous educational opportunities to be experienced in your college career, even at one institution. From studying abroad to online courses offered by other universities or even spending a semester at another school, the possibilities are limited only by oneself. The best way to discover what is available is to do your own research and learn how those offerings might best help you encounter the subjects and experiences you desire.

One last thing for you to keep in mind throughout your college journey: It is likely that you will need some help at some point during your studies, and whatever it is that you need, there is probably a free or low-cost service available on your campus. Schools have everything from free tutoring, free or low-cost medical clinics, and counseling services to cheap laundry facilities. And beyond your *needs*, there are generally other quality facilities like gyms, weight rooms, pools, and sports courts (basketball, volleyball, racquetball, etc.) at your disposal.

One thing is for certain: College is the adventure of a lifetime! It can present some of the very best and conversely some of the most difficult situations for a newly independent person to face. But to quote Tom Hanks in the film *A League of Their Own,* "It is the hard that makes it great."

While it is my hope that your college years are mostly highs, the potential for the heights and depths of human experience is what can make this experience such an exhilarating and exciting adventure.

Welcome to the journey of entering college!

PART 1 : BEFORE YOU GO

"This might be the biggest issue that I want to communicate to college freshman. They only have one chance to be in college, and these four years go quickly. This is their time. This is one of the most unique experiences they will ever have. This is the time for them to be in college. I desperately encourage them to make the most of it. It kills me that some students do not recognize what a cool opportunity this is and fully invest themselves in these four years because they will never get it back."
—Kenton, assistant director of campus life at a Christian university

College can be one of the most transformative events in a person's life. And going *away* to college is among the most significant of events in a person's second decade of life. It is an adventure like no other. Imagine embarking on a trip to the unknown. For new college students, the prePAR-

Tion for the journey to their new campuses and lives could be a bit like NASA's two space rovers, Spirit and Opportunity, headed to Mars, on their very first trip ever to the Red Planet. Read this account of that important journey:

Both rovers were launched from Cape Canaveral Air Force Station on central Florida's Space Coast. Spirit ascended in daylight on June 10, 2003. Opportunity followed with a nighttime launch on July 7 after several days of delays for repairing cork insulation.

During the cruise to Mars, Spirit made four trajectory correction maneuvers. Opportunity performed three . . . To prevent possible problems from the flares' effects on computer memory, mission controllers commanded rebooting of the rovers' computers, a capability originally planned for use on Mars but not during the cruise.

. . . With the heat-shield portion of the aeroshell pointed forward, *the spacecraft slammed into the atmosphere at about 5.4 kilometers per second (12,000 miles per hour)* . . . Spirit landed on Jan. 4, Universal Time (at 8:35 p.m. Jan. 3, Pacific Standard Time). It *bounced about 8.4 meters (27.6 feet) high.* After *27 more bounces* and then rolling, it came to a stop about 250 to 300 meters (270 to 330 yards) from its first impact. Spirit had journeyed 487 million kilometers (303 million miles).

Opportunity landed on Jan. 25, Universal Time (at 9:05 p.m. Jan. 24, Pacific Standard Time). It traveled about 200 meters (220 yards) while *bouncing 26 times* and rolling after the impact, with a 90-degree turn northward during that period. It came to rest inside a small crater. One scientist called the landing an "interplanetary hole in one."[1]

Although I'm not sure I like the landing part of the analogy—ouch!—the rest of it fits pretty well. On the way to entering college, there can be delays, course corrections, repairs, some harrowing incidents along the way, reboots needed, and your landing may or may not be described as a hole in one, but typically in the end, all is well and the rovers make it successfully.

The part you do not want to get wrong, however, after all that prePARTion and traveling, is landing at the wrong place. It is vital to start with the right end in mind. To get this right, you have to pick well in the beginning.

THOUGHTS ON A CHRISTIAN COLLEGE

I want to insert a few thoughts about the Christian college/university. If you are not attending or planning on attending a Christian school, you can skip this, but you may find yourself in one just the same. This happens every year at the Christian university at which I teach. Whether because of personal choice, opportunity to participate in collegiate sports, pressure from family, or other circumstances, you find yourself enrolled in a Christian college/university. Let's talk about what that means and why. First, let's define

1. NASA Website, Mars Rover Fact Sheet. *http://marsrover.nasa.gov/newsroom/.* Accessed November 24, 2010, emphasis added.

what I mean when I say "Christian college." I mean an institution that is thoroughly and profoundly based upon and reflects the life of Jesus Christ. Not simply one that has roots or that was once related to a church or denomination. This means that the president or provost of the institution not only *is* a Christian but sees his or her faith and the exercise of his or her role as leader of the institution as intertwined.

Many institutions of higher education are no longer meaningfully connected to their Christian heritage. To say it plainly, they are no longer thoroughly Christian. So be sure to investigate this reality before setting off and believing that a particular school is Christian simply because its name sounds like it is or because it has Christian roots.

I believe in a Christian education. And to operationalize that belief, I am investing my life teaching at a Christian university. We are a thoroughly Christian institution. Professors cannot teach here without confessing and maintaining a personal and transforming relationship with Jesus Christ. Our president is deeply committed not only to our faith heritage but also our denominational and theological heritage as well. The faculty and staff across the campus are deeply committed Christian persons.

To create a Christian *ethos* in such an institution can be a tricky reality to realize, however. Not everyone who comes to a Christian university to receive an education *is* a Christian. (This is actually a good thing, by the way, and helps keep the classrooms and the campus based in an outside-the-classroom reality.) But, given this actuality, how does an entire campus community feel Christian and practice a rhythm of life together (because Christianity is not an individual sport, after all, but about a community of faith and a body of believers)? Does the administration simply provide venues like weekly chapel services, prayer and spiritual emphases, opportunities to serve, mission trips, worship experiences, etc., and then hope that the campus community takes part? Or are some of these experiences required? It is difficult to create a unified campus and a thoroughly Christian one without at least some baseline expectations of everyone who is a part of the campus.

For this reason many colleges and universities that are committed to being and remaining Christian enact certain requirements like mandatory chapel attendance, lifestyle contracts, and Bible and theology courses in the general education requirements. For us on the campus of the university I work for, it means chapel attendance is required for all campus personnel (students, faculty, and administrators) weekly on Monday mornings. (Chapel is also offered on Wednesday and Friday mornings as well but is not required for all campus personnel. Students are required to attend a certain number of chapels each semester.) This is a time for the whole campus to be together, worship together, and grow in faith together, which is a fitting and proper thing for Christians to do (see Hebrews 10:24-25).

Without these requirements, how else would a campus community practice what they say they believe? We also all commit to living life together with some baseline commitments, such as how we deal with the issue of alcohol as a campus. Undoubtedly, alcohol consumption is a significant part of many people's college experiences. In some places, to attend college is nearly synonymous with being exposed to (and often partaking in) numerous opportunities of parties, often centered around kegs of beer. Unfortunately, the drinking that transpires at these parties can significantly contribute to all kinds of behaviors that are harmful to students (not to mention the illegality of many such acts, like underage drinking).

As a direct result of this reality, our campus discourages the use of alcohol as a beverage. This is one of those baseline expectations I spoke of earlier. To choose to attend our school (and many Christian schools) is to choose to commit to a lifestyle contract that states that you will not drink alcohol. Of course, before a student reaches twenty-one years of age, this ought not be a major issue, but even persons who teach on an adjunct basis are expected not to promote the use of alcohol (although they are not required to abstain themselves).

Further, to be a truly "Christian" institution means that one is making an effort at providing instruction in the primary text of followers of Jesus—the Bible. In order to make a good faith effort to introduce all students to the Bible, regardless of personal religious beliefs, many Christian schools require some basic courses in the Bible, and some include theology as well. At our institution, there are lower-division courses in Bible and theology that all students must take. The purpose is to give students a basic grasp and overview on each of these critical areas of Christian identity formation.

You may or may not find yourself agreeing with these sort of baseline expectations, but I simply ask how else can a campus community actually *be* Christian without such guidelines? For, without such strategies, a so-called Christian university would not be materially different from any other institution of higher education, and if that were the case then what would make it *Christian*? After all, the literal translation of the word we translate as *church* means "called-out ones." We are *called out* to be separate from the rest of society, to be different, to be "little Christs" (literally what it means to be a Christian) who follow in the footsteps of Jesus himself. I'm not sure how else an entire institution can endeavor to do this without some baseline strategy that directly affects how we behave.

Even though I did not attend a Christian school until I went to seminary, I understand and support these guidelines. In my own journey through several different institutions, I was exposed to many, many situations where alcohol was the source of lots and lots of unnecessary pain, heartbreak, destruction, and brokenness. Not interested in these rules? Then attend a school that does not ask you to abide by them. Just do not attend a school that does have them, and commit to abiding by them, only to flagrantly break them and then complain about the consequences. That is the most indefensible and, frankly, immature stance one could take.

FIRST THINGS FIRST

What to bring to college? The short answer is, not everything you may be thinking! Each fall, I help move freshmen into their new homes—the dorms—and sometimes when I am helping unpack the full-sized truck *and* car loaded with stuff, the thought strikes me, *I wonder if this person has any idea how small his/her room really is?* Not only are dorm rooms notoriously small; they are also typically shared with a roommate who often has the same idea about bringing every possible thing that may be needed. This is not a *bad* idea, but it is generally not necessary. To help you keep from doing what is typical—bringing way too much stuff and filling your precious real estate with redundant goods—

I will share a few tips on how to plan for setting up your dorm perfectly . . . or at least avoid bringing a bunch of needless stuff that just clutters your room.

The best first step is to find out what is already provided by the university and what kind of storage that includes. For example, sometimes there are facilities in each hall or wing of a dorm that residents can use to store seasonal equipment—like snow skis, for example. This obviously would be helpful to know before heading off to school. Generally, however, your room will have a bed, desk, a closet, and maybe a sink and mirror. Of course, some institutions set their students up in suites complete with kitchenettes and bathrooms, but you certainly want to know what your living situation will be because it will significantly influence what you bring. Dorms often have some sort of lounge on each hall that has some amenities like a microwave, TV, couch, possibly a coffee maker, and maybe a community fridge. Some dorms even have computer labs. Knowledge of the presence of these items, and particularly whether your room is near them and they are shared by a reasonable number of people, can be critical. Why spend your limited graduation money on a new microwave/TV/coffee maker, etc., if one is right across the hall from your room? I would much rather save my money for other things!

A good second step—after you have a firm grasp on what is provided for you both in your room and on your hall—is to contact the person(s) with whom you will be sharing your new living space. Your institution ought to be able to supply this contact info several weeks—sometimes even months—before you are scheduled to move in. In fact, a great way to get started in your relationship with this person is to work together to set up your room in a way that fits both of your hopes and dreams. Of course, this can be tricky too, since communicating with a person you have never met about such an important issue can present some obstacles. (Those of you who will live with someone you already know are a step ahead already!) All the same, with a little patience and flexibility, your room will be much more comfortable *without* two microwaves, two TVs, two stereo systems, etc. Getting in contact with this person early may allow you to negotiate who brings what and how best to share those kinds of items that do not need to be duplicated. Of course, something like a laptop does not fit in this category, but a microwave certainly does. Some people can be pretty possessive about their stuff—particularly if it was a graduation present or purchased with graduation money. All the more reason to deal with these kinds of issues *before* move-in day. A phone call will quickly make clear how your new roomie feels about these things and will set your expectations accordingly.

So, on what ought you spend that graduation money? I would argue that there are two items—one essential and one likely essential (depending on your school)—to consider: a laptop and a bicycle (or other equivalent person-powered form of transportation). The laptop may be a no-brainer, but I did not want to leave it out. For most students, their laptops are central to their lives on campus, not only for the obvious reasons like taking notes in class and writing papers but for communication and entertainment as well. A laptop may already have been integral to your life in these ways, but it is likely that going to college will increase your reliance on it. If you have not already made this purchase, some important elements to consider would be a relatively new device, a decent-size screen (not too big for portability but large enough so you can easily watch movies, etc.), and plenty of memory and hard-drive space.

The necessity of a bicycle (or scooter, or moped, etc.) really depends on the unique layout of your particular institution. For example, is it a long distance from one side of campus to the other, or does it require only a ten-minute walk to get across campus? What are winters like? Are they super cold, with lots of snow, thus significantly affecting what modes of transportation are realistic? Or are they mild, thus allowing bike riding all year? Consideration of these factors is clearly important, but it is likely that some form of on-campus, person-powered transportation will be needed or at least helpful.

My freshman year found me on a large university campus, and a bike was absolutely essential to getting around. I had a sweet black, single-speed beach cruiser complete with fat, white wall tires. The one thing I did not realize that first year was that college campuses are often a target for bike theft, so even though I had a super strong U lock, there was nothing to guard my back tire. One weekend I left my bike locked by the dining facility instead of in front of my dorms, and that was all it took. I found it on Monday morning with no back tire. I was not only completely bummed but late for class without it. So get some sort of dependable person-powered transportation and then a device to ensure it is there when you need it.

That is probably a good start for you. Of course, you will need appropriate clothing for each of the seasons you will experience at school, and if the climate is vastly different from what you've been used to at home, make sure you are prepared for that. Having plenty of toiletries, school supplies, snacks, etc., is also great. Just don't forget that there are stores nearby wherever your school is, so you do not necessarily need to stock up as if you are going to be on a desert island.

GROWTH AND CHANGE

We are encountering tons of new things, so be open to changes in life and beliefs. I think it's important to realize how much of a new beginning this can be for your life."
—Aaron, college freshman

In many ways, college is about 10% classroom and 90% living life, figuring out who you are. College can be a place for new beginnings spiritually, academically, etc. However, without intentional changes, poor habits and behaviors will follow you to college."

—University professor

I want to help you understand this stage of life you are now in called late adolescence or emerging adulthood.[2] A growing number of developmental psychologists claim that this is a new part of the human life cycle that has been

---

2. Arnett, Jeffrey Jensen. *Emerging Adulthood: The Winding Road from the Late Teens Through the Twenties.* New York: Oxford University Press, 2004.

brought on by the delay of the classic markers of adulthood: full-time employment, marriage, and child rearing.[3]

Aaron says it well. College freshmen "are encountering tons of new things." In addition, for the freshman who is coming to college right after high school (or within a year or so of high school graduation) s/he has also entered a new stage of life. The teen years are quickly evaporating into memories, and the unknown twenties stretch before them. Jeffrey Jensen Arnett argues that there are not the clear pathways to adulthood there once were.

For example, in the past, a person could graduate from high school and go right into a manufacturing job in the U.S. Perhaps that job would be in the automotive industry or the textile industry or the steel industry. These kinds of jobs were often physically demanding but paid a good wage and generally offered considerable benefits (health insurance and a pension). High school graduates worked in those industries for their entire careers—often spanning thirty or forty years or more—and then had the promise of a stable income for the rest of their lives, thanks to the pensions their employers offered. Jobs like these are all but extinct in the U.S. today.

Today the equivalent of the high school diploma of yesterday has become the bachelor's degree and is quickly becoming the master's degree. In the U.S. economy, technical and highly specialized positions (such as computer pro-

_____

3. For more on this, read Arnett's book. It is easy to understand and a helpful resource about twenty-somethings.

grammers or health care workers) are what are listed in the classifieds—not typically manufacturing or other manual-labor jobs. What does this mean for you? It means that the best thing you can find is an area of study that truly interests you enough to study it in depth. Then you will not only major in this field but ought to consider going on to graduate school to study this discipline for another two or more years.

Although this may be too much to really synthesize at this point, it is still important to keep in mind. For now, just realize this is part of the landscape you are entering as a young adult and file it away in your mind—just not too far in the back. Let's get on to something that is much more a part of your everyday life—like this idea of emerging adulthood.

Before we get into the characteristics of emerging adulthood, it might be helpful to understand what was supposed to take place during adolescence. This will help to put into proper perspective the difference between the adolescent and emerging adult. According to Chap Clark in *Starting Right: Thinking Theologically about Youth Ministry*, there are three primary tasks that the adolescent must master. They are: 1) identity, 2) autonomy, 3) reconnection.[4]

In a nutshell, the task of identity formation is about the adolescent answering the question, *Who am I?*[5] There are

---

4. Chap Clark, "The Changing Face of Adolescence: A Theological View of Human Development," in *Starting Right : Thinking Theologically about Youth Ministry,* ed. Chap Clark, David Rahn, Kenda Creasy Dean (Grand Rapids: Zondervan, 2001), 54-55.

5. Ibid, 55.

various understandings of how this process takes place that go much beyond the purpose of this chapter and book. Let it suffice to say that forming one's identity is both an outside-in process of sifting through various possibilities—sort of like trying on different styles of clothing—and an inside-out process of discovering who it is that God has created you to be (see Psalm 139).

The task of becoming autonomous or accepting responsibility for oneself is to answer the question, *Do I matter?*[6] Part of what happens in this process is for the adolescent to learn that he or she has a unique perspective to contribute. Although you may not be the smartest, fastest, or best, you have something to contribute to the group and to society as a whole. Coming to accept this is part of what it means to achieve autonomy.

The last task of adolescence is that of reconnection or belonging. This is to answer the question, *How do I relate to others?*[7] This task requires the adolescent to learn the difference and to travel the road from dependence to independence to interdependence. For a time, people may be tempted to believe they are islands, capable of doing it all themselves. The more mature response is one that recognizes the need and even necessity of others in our lives and what we contribute to the lives of others. This understanding is that of an interdependent person.

---

6. Ibid.
7. Ibid.

CHARACTERISTICS OF THE EMERGING ADULT

Dr. Jeffery Jensen Arnett, arguably the leading contemporary scholar on late adolescence and emerging adulthood, offers five distinctives of the emerging adult in his book *Emerging Adulthood: The Winding Road from the Late Teens Through the Twenties.* Arnett names these as:

1. The age of *identity explorations*, trying out various possibilities, especially in love and work;
2. The age of *instability*;
3. The most *self-focused* age of life;
4. The age of feeling *in between*, in transition, neither adolescent nor adult;
5. The age of *possibilities*, when hopes flourish, when people have an unparalleled opportunity to transform their lives.[8]

What do you think on first look? Do these characteristics fit you? Let's unpack them a bit before you decide. I'll do my best to illustrate what these characteristics look like by providing some real-life situations of emerging adults I know (without using their real names, of course).

The age of identity explorations. It was discovered that is it developmentally typical for the emerging adult to exhibit a shopping-around attitude with regard to work, often changing jobs several times in a search for the perfect job. The "perfect job" is defined as employment that enables

---

8. Arnett, 8 (emphasis added).

emerging adults to express their unique identity, help make them better people, and do some good for others. This behavior—changing jobs often—is sometimes described as floundering, although Arnett claims it is an intentional search and exploration of their identity. Nevertheless, once hired, it is uncommon for an emerging adult to stay put in a particular job for more than a year or two.

Tim is a good example of this sort of exploration. Tim is in his early twenties, a fifth-year youth ministry major. He recently turned down a valuable youth ministry opportunity in a solid local church where he had been working for the past three years. Instead of completing his formal internship (required for graduation) at this church while being compensated relatively well (small salary, housing, expense account, health insurance, and even retirement) he felt that he was not called to local church youth ministry and decided to find another church in which to complete his internship requirement. Why would he do such a thing, potentially delaying graduation and turning down a chance to learn from an established youth minister? There was no obvious reason for Tim to move; his relationships with students, parents, and other church staff were good. So is Tim searching or floundering? Who knows?

The age of instability. The primary expression of this characteristic is a relatively high number of residence changes per year. The main reason for this is the exploratory nature of emerging adulthood. Although not previously stated, another way to express instability would seem to be restlessness or even discontent. This characteristic is visible in Tanya.

Tanya graduated more than a year ago with a degree in youth ministry. She is a bright, attractive, intelligent young woman. The first year she was out of college, she decided she did not want to take a full-time ministry position but would rather put herself in an intentional situation of mentoring with an experienced youth minister while working part time. She found an excellent situation with a seasoned and thoughtful youth minister who took her on as an apprentice. Although she enjoyed their relationship and being involved in ministry at that church, she decided after a couple of months that it was not a good fit and stopped attending there or any church regularly after that. She held down three part-time jobs to survive and felt generally lost as far as what was next for her. Next summer she plans on going to Taiwan to teach English for one year. When she returns, she has no idea what she will do or where she will live.

The most self-focused age of life. Mark was elated with his newfound freedom. During his first year of college, he attended a community college not far from his home. Throughout that year he continued to live with his parents and work the same part-time job he had during high school. Not much had changed from his senior year of high school.

The next year, however, Mark attended a four-year university five hundred miles away from his family and lived off campus. He relished that he could do anything he wanted. The only rules that existed were self-imposed. Although he loved and respected his parents, he was also fond of late-night gatherings at his apartment, discussing Nietzsche's philosophy with his classmates, and German beer. Even better were the nights that these three intersected. None of these things would have met with the approval of his parents, who were extremely conservative. However, Mark felt it was his responsibility to push his traditional boundaries so he could grow up. After all, his parents had raised him in a sheltered environment, and he mused, *Isn't this what college life is all about?* Although this self-focus is not selfishness, *per se*, but rather a direct result of the freedom accompanying emerging adulthood and the requisite self-determination of this period, emerging adults often exhibit, in the words of Sharon Parks, a "fragile inner-dependence"[9] that expresses a growing self-trust but not one fully developed.

The age of feeling in between. When asked, most emerging adults see the age of thirty as the marker for adulthood. Relativistic thinking also contributes to this feeling where all choices and paths appear to be equally valid. The product of this kind of stage can be seen in Tina. She graduated recently spring with a liberal arts degree with an emphasis in graphic arts. Although Tina is capable and possesses a deep inner composure, she lives with her parents and does not know what she will do next. She has been offered some significant positions by various organizations. These opportunities are attractive to her but also scary. She is afraid she might pick the wrong one. She seems to enjoy

9. Sharon Daloz Parks. *Big Questions, Worthy Dreams: Mentoring Young Adults in Their Search for Meaning, Purpose, and Faith* (San Francisco: Jossey-Bass, 2000), 73.

talking about work in the adult world while going home each night and sleeping in the bed, in the home, of her adolescence.

The age of possibilities. This distinctive is contributed to by the wide range of choices before emerging adults "more than ever before or than ever will be again." This is a time that emerging adults can pursue their dreams, and many do throughout their third decade of life. For example, take Alejandro; he was one of those students who was easy to like. He was smart, had a great sense of humor, exhibited respect, and loved playing baseball at the university level. Toward the end of his senior year, I spoke with him about what was next. He said with a large smile, "I hope to be able to continue in baseball." I asked if he had been recruited by a professional scout or if he was he going to try out for a local minor league team? Neither had occurred. He just hoped something might work out.

Arnett contrasts this understanding of emerging adulthood with the top three criteria of full adulthood, which are:

1. Accepting responsibility for oneself.

2. Making independent decisions.

3. Becoming financially independent.[10]

Here we have the top three commonly viewed characteristics that indicate they have moved from the twenty-something emerging adult to actual adulthood. It is a pretty good list too. Most college students (or even college-aged persons) are getting some financial help from parents or

---

10. Ibid, 15.

other relatives. According to twenty-somethings themselves, these are the marks of full adulthood. Other items that did not make the top three but have been historic markers of adulthood are marriage, having children, and completing one's education.[11]

Although written specifically about American college students in a national study, Jennifer Lindholm's words seem fitting as a summary for the phase of life discussed here as emerging adulthood. Lindholm writes:

'What am I going to do with my life?' . . . 'What kind of person do I want to be?' 'How is everything I've worked for up to this point going to contribute back to society?' . . . These were (among) the life questions noted most frequently by undergraduate students. . . . For traditional-age college students, the undergraduate years are commonly characterized as an intensive period of cognitive, social, and affective development. As they refine their identities, formulate adult life goals and career paths, test their emerging sense of self-authority and interdependence, and make decisions that will significantly impact their own and others' lives . . .[12]

THE BOTTOM LINE

The point in sharing all of this is to do two things. The first is to impress upon you the excitement and adventure

11. Ibid, 210.

12. Lindholm, Jennifer A. "The Interior Lives of American College Students: Preliminary Findings from a National Study." In *Passing on the Faith,* edited by James L. Heft, 75-102. New York: Fordham University Press, 2006, 75.

of heading off to college while stressing the importance of finding a school that has the right fit. It is a new beginning and a quest unlike any other you have taken up to this point in your life, and being in the right place is crucial. This is supposed to get you stoked—not stressed! You are going to encounter incredible new people, ideas, learning, and decisions that will shape the rest of your life. Framing it in those terms is not meant to intimidate you (although it is difficult not to be intimidated by these decisions) but rather to pump you up for the exploration ahead. For each of us, going to college is a bit like going to Mars: completely unknown but very exciting!

The second goal of this section of this book has been to introduce you to this new part of the human life cycle you are entering and how it is different from adolescence. It is a period that is completely foreign to your parents and other relatives. Although they were at one time in their late teens and twenties, they did not experience emerging adulthood and the situation we are now in as a global community that has created this new part of the human life cycle. For this reason they may struggle to understand all of what you are experiencing, the pressures you feel, and the reality of the job market today. That does not mean you cannot talk to them; they are your greatest allies, and you need them and other adults in your life; it is just meant to help structure your understanding accordingly.

PART 2:
STARTING WELL

"Don't get hung up on friends or boyfriends/
girlfriends from back home. The other
freshmen I know who did are the ones who
aren't that connected with hardly anyone
because all they do is sit in their rooms on
the phone, Facebook, or Skype."
—Megan, college freshman

"Relationships. This is another huge issue.
I think there are two sides of it. The first
is when students come to college with
girlfriends or boyfriends back home. This
can completely hamper their freshman year.
They are going to change so much during
their freshman year at college. Usually these
relationships end over Christmas break or
the next summer. And those students have
lost a ton of time during their freshman year
that they could have been involved more with
college. Second, so many college freshmen
feel like they have to have a girlfriend or

boyfriend right away. Now that they are in college, for some odd reason, they feel like they have to date. Nope. Just hang out. Just have fun. Don't worry about it."

—Kenton, assistant director of campus life at a Christian university

In the movie *Father of the Bride* there is a great scene that takes place the night before Annie is to be married. Her father, George, wakes up in the middle of the night to the sound of a bouncing basketball. George investigates and finds Annie shooting hoops in the middle of the night. When he asks Annie what is going on, Annie talks about being restless because of the huge life change that is about to take place. She talks about how the bedroom of her childhood room, where she was attempting to sleep, will no longer be hers, and although she is excited for the future, she's not quite ready to let go. George confides to her that he is struggling with the same things. Just at this moment it starts to snow, which triggers happy memories for each of them. They share a special moment together and seem to realize that change is a part of life and that all will be all right in the end.[13]

Going to college can be a lot like this experience. There is a great sense of excitement and anticipation for what is

13. Fields, Doug and Eddie James. *Videos that Teach*. Zondervan: Grand Rapids, MI. 1999.

ahead. Simultaneously, there might be reluctance for what will be left behind. Actually arriving on your new campus can elicit a mix of feelings from complete abandonment by your family to the greatest sense of freedom and exploration you have ever experienced. My hope for you is that it is more of the latter and less of the former. One thing is for sure, however: You, just like Annie, will likely return to the home of your childhood, but it will never be quite the same home again. This important step into college signals a significant change of status on your road to adulthood. You are no longer a child living safely in your parents' house. In fact, you may come to find that your home becomes more and more closely associated with where you go to college than that of the town where your parents live.

Move-in day in the dorms ought to be a lot of fun. For one thing, you're meeting tons of new people who are *all* feeling a mix of emotions, just like you. It can be helpful to remember that. Regardless of how calm others may appear, this is a wonderful *and* difficult day for everyone. As a professor, I now have the privilege of helping our freshmen move into the dorms. Our entire university community comes out to welcome new students, talk to parents, and help carry the incalculable mounds of stuff into the small dorm rooms. We love move-in day around here. Our university does all it can to make those first few hours of transition to our campus fun, pain free, and welcoming. I have learned a lot through reflecting on these experiences, watching literally thousands of new freshmen arrive on campus and move in and remembering my own move-in day story.

How you leave home, in terms of prePARTion, saying goodbye to friends, and even how early you start packing and how much sleep you get can make a significant difference in how you arrive. My own move-in day experience was not very good; actually, it was a disaster! I did *a lot* of things wrong without realizing it at the time. Although pretty embarrassing, I'll share some of this experience with you in hopes that you will avoid the same mistakes I made.

Wanting to leave well, I planned an elaborate last date with my girlfriend. She was planning on staying at home and attending the local community college. I was going about five hundred miles away to a large university of about eighteen thousand undergrads and feeling like it was the end of my life. Since I was an eighteen-year-old in love, I felt as if those five hundred miles were the equivalent of going to the moon. If you saw how much angst and sorrow both of us had that evening, you might think I was going off to war!

The date I planned that night involved having a wonderful take-out dinner (I couldn't cook) that I set up at sunset on this beautiful butte overlooking the Sacramento River. I spent the entire day getting ready, instead of packing for college as I should have been doing (actually, I ought to have been already done with packing so I could enjoy this last night in town). I thought of everything that night, from candles on the white linen tablecloth to a personalized mix tape (as in, cassette) that I played during the entire date and then gave to my girlfriend at the end of the night. I was clearly thinking about this date and not thinking about going to college, even though my parents and I would leave early the next morning to make the five-hundred-mile drive.

The date went well. The setting was beautiful, the food good, and there were lots of promises and expressions of our undying devotion to one another. I'll call this mistake #1. We stayed out late that night. Mistake #2. When I did finally get home, I still had to pack. Mistake #3! My girlfriend, who lived about an hour outside of town, ended up just coming to my house that night rather than driving home at 1:00 a.m. Mistake #4. She crashed out on the couch, and I started packing. I took trip after trip from my room out to my parents' car. On my last trip out, I heard my parents' alarm go off, meaning it was time to get up and begin the trip. I had been up all night. Mistake #5. I was exhausted. Mistake #6. I was emotionally drained (all those expressions of my undying love!). Mistake #7. And, although I was packed, my belongings were not packed with any sense of order, so you could say both my stuff and I were a mess. Mistake #8.

Did I mention I made *a lot* of mistakes? Needless to say, the trip did not go smoothly. Before my parents and I could even leave, I had to say goodbye (for the hundredth time!) to my girlfriend, and that meant we not only ended our evening in tears, we began our day in tears as well; not smart! I got in my parents' car feeling like I would rather not go to college ever; not a great way to begin a five-hundred-mile drive that is supposed to be a fun time with my parents and a closing chapter on childhood. I was pretty miserable the entire ten hours, and my parents probably were too. I alternated between sleeping and being generally irritable for most of the trip in the backseat of the car. Fun, eh?

I can't imagine what the people thought who helped unpack my belongings. I must have looked pretty bad—tear swollen and sleep deprived—and my parents were likely very happy when the last load was taken out of their car. They hugged me and left—maybe escaped is more like what they felt at the time. I felt terribly abandoned and alone. My girlfriend was five hundred miles away, my parents just left, I did not know a soul in the seven-story dorm I had just moved into, and my roommate was not there yet. I was one sad little puppy.

Could this disaster have been avoided? Maybe not completely, but the torture I chose to put myself through could have been significantly decreased.

LEAVING WELL

Leaving well is a skill anyone can learn, but it seems that so few endeavor to. It is primarily about being intentional with the choices you make, particularly as you near the end of your summer before college. This only requires you to consider how your relationships and choices will affect you (and others) as you go off to college. Obviously the situation will be different if you are not going away to college, but it still applies. How you finish your high school years matters, and the summer prior to starting college is the boundary between the two experiences that can seem like two absolutely different lives.

My first piece of advice is aimed at those of you who—like I was—are in a serious romantic relationship. It is critical that you talk with your significant other about how you are going to deal with the move to college. Even if you are both going to the same school, it is still important that this conversation occurs. It is not prudent to just suppose that everything will remain as it has. It likely will not because a major transition is about to take place. You need to search your own heart about your desires for the relationship and future and allow your boy/girl friend to do the same. It is vital that you are both honest about your feelings with yourselves and each other. Clear and open communication is key here.

My unsolicited advice is to consider the possibility of dating other people. I know this can sound like death itself to some of you (frankly, it would have to me), but this one decision could make the difference between a good start and a horrible start to your college experience. Like Megan says at the beginning of this chapter, a boy/girl friend at home can act like an obstacle to developing new friendships (even platonic ones).

There seems to be some mysterious but true law of the college universe that when a person is in a serious relationship with someone living in another place, that person clings to that relationship rather than developing new ones. It is as if s/he feels guilty for having fun. It is strange but often what happens and can be destructive to new relationships. It is like people feel they are being unfaithful if they even enjoy other people's company. It sounds crazy, but that's what I did, it's what Megan is seeing, and it is all too typical. (Because of this reality I once chose to do my laundry one Saturday night over hanging out with some high school friends who had come down to my campus. Why? Because I once liked one of the girls who was visiting and felt that might somehow be unfair to my girlfriend back home.) Even though you may intend not to do this, it is a common error. The bottom line is, talk it over with your boy or girlfriend, and at the very least, *consider* dating other people. Whatever you do, be aware of this common pitfall.

Second, spend quality time with people you will miss. These people may be friends, teachers, coaches, or relatives. Be intentional about having last conversations with them. It may be a coffee date or less formal—like, just a short but meaningful stand-up conversation. It does not need to take long, but you need to do three things. 1) Express to them what they have meant to you. 2) Tell them thanks. 3) Say goodbye. It lets them know they meant something to you and allows you to leave knowing you ended a relationship well. Although it may not actually be the end of the relationship, unless you are good at keeping in contact with all of these folks, it may be a long while before you connect again.

For example, I had a football and track coach throughout high school who meant the world to me. He was one of those adults in my world who made a difference. Not only was he my coach for two sports a year; he got me my first job. There was scarcely a day I did not spend with Coach after school on the practice field or in the weight room.

He was my friend and a mentor. He believed in me and invested in my life. Because of this, I just assumed we'd keep in touch. I imagined stopping by my old high school on a break from college and seeing Coach around. It never happened. I had the best intentions, but it just never happened. In fact, I just finally sat down with my old coach a year ago—more than twenty years after I graduated from high school! If there are folks you need to say thanks and goodbye to, do it before you leave. Even if it means you have to write it in a card because you don't have the time; just do it.

As you can see, leaving well typically involves relationships. It is about not leaving things unsaid and clarifying expectations for the road ahead. It is about giving people the proper respect and thanks they deserve. It also means respecting yourself enough not to be tied down to a relational commitment you may not really be that into. If that is the case, the most loving and grace-filled thing you can do is set that person free. There are many other things that could be said about leaving well, like not waiting to pack until the last minute, not packing too much, cleaning your room, and not leaving it looking like it was ransacked for your folks, etc., but I think you've got the picture.

ROOMMATE(S)

Likely one of the first new people you will meet besides all the folks helping carry your stuff up to your new home will be your roommate. This is a very important person in your life, so treat him or her well. After all, you will be living together for the next nine months. Even more than that, this will be the person you come home to at night to talk about your day and to process both wonderful and difficult things you experience on this new venture. Normally colleges and universities do their very best to match roommates well. After all, the college administration wants you to stay. Right? There are informational surveys that most send out to incoming students that, if filled out accurately, reveal habits and preferences that should help them match you with a good fit. Even with this information, however, matching two different people to share a small space can be difficult. Having a good relationship with any roommate requires three things: adaptation, flexibility, and clear communication. And these also apply if this roommate is a friend you have known for a while.

Ideally, your roommate will share many of your same habits and preferences. For instance, they will (just like you) prefer to sleep in late on Saturday mornings but not stay up too late during the week because they are good students and get up by 6:30 a.m. each day to study or work out. They will never leave dirty laundry on the floor or dirty dishes with rotting food in your room. They will be respectful when they come home late and not turn on your room light but just use a nightlight to get ready for bed. They will be careful not to let the door slam when you are studying or sleeping but will always be glad to share their iPod and speakers with you. The ideal roommate will make their bed each morning and generally keep the room clean in case friends come over to visit. They will not snore or talk in their sleep and never allow their alarm to go off and use more than one snooze. In general, this roommate will be respectful and pleasant, helpful and kind, and act like a sibling in the very best sense of the word—just like you. Right?

On the other hand, your roommate may be quite different from you. They may get up at 5:00 a.m. every day because they are modest and don't want to shower with anyone else around. They may refuse to ever undress when you are around. They may not want you to touch their stuff and may even put a piece of tape down the middle of the room dividing your side from their side (Sound childish? It happens, trust me). They may be a complete neat freak with the exception of one flaw, being that they never wash dishes until they smell so bad they are literally growing mold and mildew. They may hate your friends and be so rude as to talk on the phone about you and them when you are around. Your roommate could decide to go to bed each night at 9:00 p.m. and expect you to be silent when in the room . . . You get my drift? There are no guarantees when you are matched up with a roommate, thus the need to be adaptable, flexible, and able to communicate about your needs and wants.

Adaptability is a critical characteristic because living with someone requires you not to expect everything to be as you want it. For example, your new roomie may love country music, and you only like classic rock. Time to be adaptable and maybe even to learn to appreciate at least *some* country music. This also requires flexibility and good communication to negotiate when and what kind of music is going to be played (if any) when you are both in the room. Flexibility is also a key trait for roommates because life often requires that we bend to accommodate one another. As long as both roommates are flexible, all is well. If one is ever the primary person responsible for flexing, something is bound to break (eventually maybe the relationship itself).

This is a perfect time for a little lesson in assertiveness and active listening—a valuable set of skills for any relationship. Assertiveness is the ability to ask for what you want or need. Being assertive does not involve manipulation or guilt. It is simply about clearly and unequivocally asking or stating what you want to occur in any situation. For example, if your roommate has a habit of leaving dirty laundry on the floor until it finally grows legs and crawls away and that is a cause of concern for you? Acting in an assertive manner means having a conversation with your roomie and saying something like the following: "I would really appreciate it if you would put your dirty laundry in the laundry bag in your closet and keep it off the floor of our room." See what happened here? You did not hint around at the issue but clearly came out and asked for what you wanted. Generally, if this kind of clear communication takes place, results occur.

Active listening is the other side of assertiveness. Active listening ensures that the message that is being sent is being received. So let's go back to the example about the dirty laundry above. If the roomie were to practice active listening, after hearing your request, they would repeat back the message by saying something like, "I understand that you do not appreciate my dirty laundry on the floor of our room and would like me to place it in my closet." That would ensure that they heard what you actually said. That is a good thing, right? Now, hopefully they actually do it! Although most people don't speak like this in everyday communication, what is important is to ensure that the messages we send are received by the ones we send them to. This kind of communication is vital with roommates, close friends, and particularly with significant others. Keep it in mind because, even if you are the only one being assertive and listening actively, it can have a huge effect on the relationship.

The upshot here is to have the courage to express your feelings if things are not going so well, clearly ask for what you want, and then be flexible and adaptable to negotiate a workable solution.

NEW FRIENDS

"Find a group of friends that can be a support group, that you can talk about things ranging from what you learned in class to problems you're having on a personal level."
—Aaron, college freshman

New friendships are the lifeblood of the college experience. These new relationships will not only be the source of much fun, growth, and discovery, but they will also serve a crucial role of support on your college journey. I will never forget two of my best friends during my freshman year. Jud and Jason were an absolute Godsend to me. They befriended me, included me, and helped me in my newfound faith as a follower of Jesus Christ. They were both men of strong faith—although I had grown up in a quasi-Christian home, my faith life was a relatively new thing. None of us had known one another before arriving on campus, but we were fast friends. They were both on my hall in the dorm; we were all just a couple of doors apart from one another. I remember having the experience of feeling like I had two good friends nearly from the moment I arrived on campus. There is nothing better than that feeling, especially when it is so easy to feel vulnerable and alone those first few days.

When any of us headed to the dining commons at mealtime, we first sought out the others to come along. Sometimes just having someone to sit with at lunch or dinner can provide such comfort. Those times can be the loneliest, especially if your family ate together at home. But our friendship extended much beyond eating together. We all joined a small group Bible study that met in our dorm. We attended church together. We spent our weekends together. And, perhaps most importantly, we shared our hopes, disappointments, successes, and failures with one another. It was Jud and Jason who helped me break the bad habit of cussing that I brought to college. It was Jason who selflessly lent me his car to drive around when my girlfriend came to visit. It was these two friends who helped me in innumerable ways to solidify my shaky faith. They did this in part by being faithful followers of Jesus.

My advice is to be kind to everyone you meet. You will likely not end up hanging out with everyone, but you certainly do not need to alienate anyone. It is natural to gravitate toward others with whom you share common interests, but in being kind to and making friends with everyone, you will never be far from a person to whom you can talk. And you may be surprised the strange twists and turns that life can take during college. One of the persons on your dorm hall who might not be a natural friend may end up being one of your very closest friends in the future. Besides, why would you want to ever alienate another? There is just no good reason to do so.

The friends who are here at school are a vital support network. The best thing you can do is invest time and emotional energy in them. If you are so invested in relationships at home and attempting to stay connected with them through Facebook, texting, email, etc., then it will be much more difficult to develop close relationships at college. I made that mistake my freshman year and I really regretted it. Although I did have friends like Jason and Jud, I disabled my own ability to cultivate new friends due to my constant focus on my girlfriend back at home.

An example of how I sabotaged myself in forming new friends happened during that year. I was in an Introduction to Theater course, and one of the requirements was to attend several local plays and performances. Our class, although large, quickly formed spontaneous smaller groups of ten or so students who banded together to travel and endure or enjoy (depending upon the particular play) the productions together. I ended up traveling regularly with a particular girl in my class. She was cool, fun, smart, and friendly. She even sought me out in the commons to talk about the recent play we had seen on a couple of occasions. What could have been a delightful new friendship I did not invest myself in because I created some crazy thought that being friends with this girl somehow translated to unfaithfulness to my girlfriend back at home. What a big mistake!

Although my girlfriend was a great person, my incessant thought about her and our relationship became a real anchor to my own growth. It was like my little brain could not deal with any more relational connections because of how deeply I felt about her—strange but true. Do not misunderstand me on this important point. It was not her fault but my own. Because of my inability or unwillingness to grow new friendships at school, I would likely have been much better off either staying at home or ending the relationship with my girlfriend. I know that may sound harsh, but it is true in my situation because I allowed the relationship to have such power in my life that it ruined my first year of college—a minor tragedy (notice I did not say *she* ruined my first year but rather the *relationship,* which I could not properly balance).

That is a year of my life and college experience I can never do again. It may or may not be true in your situation and relationship. But, like I have said before, if you are in a relationship that you plan to continue as you go off to college, clear communication is critical for everyone's health and sanity.

The point here is to reinforce the importance of blooming where you are planted. To say it another way, you need to be present to the persons and relationships that are right in front of you. Do not make the same mistake I did by missing out on new friendships because you are so focused on the old. There is a song from my childhood that seems appropriate here, due to its excellent advice. It goes like this: "Make new friends, but keep the old; one is silver and the other gold."

There are plenty more facets of new friendships that could be covered here, from Greek organizations (fraternities and sororities), campus clubs, ministry organizations, and academic societies (and I will offer some bit of advice on those in the postscript section), but overall, I have expressed my advice here. Be kind to everyone, and never, never burn a bridge with a potential friend. It is a better way to live, and who knows what may become of that relationship in the months and years to come?

FRESHMAN ORIENTATION

"Don't skip the freshman orientation just because you think it's awkward. To tell you the truth, it *is* awkward, but everyone else is awkward too."

—Chelsea, university freshman

Yes, the freshman orientation can be awkward, but it can also be the source of really helpful and even important information about life on campus. Like Chelsea suggests, do not skip it; rather, make the best of it. Freshman orientation is designed to shorten the learning curve to life on your new campus. You do not want to miss this, even if it means you have to endure some talk about male/female relationships and what is considered okay and not okay in terms of campus policies and dorm life. There will inevitably be heaps of information without which, you may be figuratively or even literally lost. So go to the freshman orientation and make the most of it. In the end it will likely prove to be indispensible.

Another indispensible act in starting off your freshman year well is getting to know the campus and surrounding area like the back of your hand. Not only do you need to know exactly where your classes meet (especially if it is a larger campus) and where to find a good burrito or cup of coffee, but you need to learn the campus lingo quickly. Every community has its own language, and a university campus is its own unique community. In all probability there will be scores of acronyms, abbreviations, and insider names for buildings, areas of campus, and even some professors. For example, on our campus, one of our professors is known as Mad Dog, and one of our buildings is known as The God Building. Although all this new information can be overwhelming at first, do not fear—your freshman orientation will aid in the process of discovering and learning these swiftly.

My recommendation for you after attending freshman orientation is to spend some time walking or riding (depending on the size) around campus to discover the best routes to get from your dorm to the various locations that your day will take you. For example, it may be easy to get to the dining commons and your classes, but can you get from your classes to the dining commons and then to the gym? For smaller campuses, this may be unnecessary, but if you on a campus with a population of 5,000 or more, it will prove helpful. There is nothing worse than being late to class on the first day because you could not find the room, even though you knew the building. I had a class that met in a large, multi-storied building my freshman year. The first day of class I discovered that, although I knew correctly where the building was, the classroom was in a strange location because it was an annex to the original building. So although it was classified as part of the original building, its location was actually outside the building in the back.

That reality made for an unnecessarily stressful first day. Do yourself a favor and do not find just your building, but locate your classrooms ahead of time as well.

Another important part of knowing your campus and local community is discovering the favorite hangouts around town. These are often places that are supportive of college students (due in part to college students' support of these businesses) and offer discounted or inexpensive meals, later hours (for studying), or just plain great food or large portions for reasonable prices. In one of my college towns, one of these places was Kona's Canoes (the canoe was a large, freshly made wheat pita pocket that was filled with a variety of chopped and steamed items of your choosing). Kona's had the most excellent sandwiches for about four dollars. There was always a college student in that place, no matter the time of day, it seemed. The food was excellent, inexpensive, and fast. There is a Kona's equivalent in *your* college town—you just have to find it. Frequently the best way to learn about some of these places is from other students—especially upper-class students.

A third dimension of learning your campus is becoming familiar with the menu of services the campus offers students. Among these services commonly are things like tutoring services, medical clinics, counseling staff, recreation centers, career and employment services, multicultural organizations, technical support, computer labs, and campus security, just to name a few. This non-exhaustive list does not include the many student-run organizations that also exist on campus. Although many of these services are no to low cost, you can rest assured that you are paying for them through your tuition and student fees. I say this not to take the luster off of them being offered but rather to encourage you to use them because, after all, *you* are paying for them. It is a strange reality to me that so many students on college campuses are either ignorant of the vast array of campus services or just choose not to take advantage of them.

Your school is probably well equipped to help you with whatever you encounter during college. No matter how serious your need or issue, in all likelihood, the school has dealt with it before. Keep this in mind: The administration at your school wants you to be successful in college and life. When you are, you are the very best advertisement for their institution. So get to know your campus and take advantage of all it has to offer.

PART 3:
FIRST SEMESTER

"Find a balance between fun and homework. College is not only about having fun; it is also where you go to prepare for your future, including your intellectual future."
—Chelsea, university freshman

Life is an opportunity, benefit from it.
Life is beauty, admire it.
Life is bliss, taste it.
Life is a dream, realize it.
Life is a challenge, meet it.
Life is a duty, complete it.
Life is a game, play it.
Life is a promise, fulfill it.
Life is a sorrow, overcome it.
Life is a song, sing it.
Life is a struggle, accept it.
Life is a tragedy, confront it.
Life is an adventure, dare it.
Life is luck, make it.
Life is too precious, do not destroy it.
Life is life, fight for it.
—Mother Teresa[14]

14. Inspiration Peak. *http://www.inspirationpeak.com/inspirational-quotes.html.* Accessed January 13, 2011.

At this point, you have already been through a lot. Think about how, just a few months back, you were in the middle of this huge decision about which school to pick, and now you are living in your new dorm room, have figured out some basics of campus life, and are meeting all kinds of new people. What you are now experiencing is going to be your life for the next few years. Like the reference from Mother Teresa above, you are liable to experience the gamut of what life offers while in college. Allow these experiences to be what they are. Try not to make them any more or less than that. What I mean is, live. Cry when it hurts, laugh when it's funny, and in all things, try to enjoy this terrific ride of college life!

Although the college experience has already begun, you haven't even been to class yet. Although the academic side is only a part of the whole college experience, it is an awfully important part. In fact, if you do not maintain a certain level of proficiency in this area, you will not be allowed to participate in sports or many other campus activities. Ultimately, if you do not maintain a certain grade point average (GPA), usually a 2.0 or better, then you will not be able to graduate.

So, although the academic side of college really is maybe only 10 percent, it is a crucial 10 percent! And it is this 10 percent that allows you to participate in the other 90 percent. Further, it is the 10 percent that your parents are likely most interested in as well—and the part that will lead to a diploma. However, the totality of the college experience can be so personally transformative—both the academic and the personal—that it can be difficult at times to understand where one ends and the next begins. Especially when you are in a class you love, you can find yourself thinking, talking, even reading about issues related to that topic that are not assigned—imagine that. You just discover that you really love this stuff! Is that schoolwork, or is that the personal side? When these two blur, then you know you have gotten your money's worth and, more importantly, that you are really learning.

PROFESSORS AND CLASS

"Get to know your professors; you may be surprised to find they are kind of cool."
—Kenneth, college freshman

Remember being in elementary school and seeing your teacher at a store or other place besides at school? Do you remember thinking, *Wow, that's Mrs. Wheeler, what is she doing here?* Perhaps you even spoke to your teacher and verbalized something similar to what you were thinking and thus revealing that it had never actually occurred to you that he or she had a life outside the classroom.

This is both kind of cute and kind of embarrassing to realize now, but it happened to so many of us that it is not all that uncommon. Just don't make the same mistake now that you are in college. Although your professors have a fair amount of power in the classroom, they are people too, and generally speaking, they are not out to get you but rather deeply desire to help you learn and succeed as students and people. At least until they prove otherwise, believe the very best about the people who serve as your college professors. This is simply the right foot to get started on in your new relationships with them.

The first rule of thumb about the college classroom: *It is different from high school.* Professors are generally more educated in their fields than typical high school teachers, but they may not be the best *teachers*. High school teachers have to have credentials and training in lesson planning and learning styles. This usually ensures they are adequate *teachers*. This is not necessarily the case in colleges and universities. The folks who teach in these settings are usually identified as experts in their fields, due to education and experience, so they know a great deal. The ironic reality is that, although they are filled with knowledge, they may never have learned well how best to pass on that knowledge to college students. If they have been teaching for several years, they have likely learned a great deal about the art of teaching, but they may still struggle in some areas to be excellent. Understanding this can help you as a student.

Part of your job is not only to study the subject you are focused on in your courses but also become a student of your professors. I do not mean to stalk them or spy on them; I just mean get to know them and learn a bit about them. Think well about who they are, how they communicate, what they expect, what is important to them, and how best to satisfy their requirements. This is important because you will begin to understand what they find most important about the subjects they teach, and this will translate not only into a better experience for you but likely better grades.

WAYS OF KNOWING

Just before we get into some of the nuts and bolts of the college classroom and how to not only survive but thrive as a new student, I am going to provide you with an important point of view about your new professors—all of them. Different professors at your school likely do not all see the world in the same way. Each has a different perspective on reality and how to answer the major questions of our time such as, *What is true?* and, *What is the meaning of life?* Although that may sound a bit cliché, it is accurate. This is due in part to their academic training. This is not to say that their perspectives are incompatible with one another; they are just different, and understanding this will go a long way toward helping you as their student.

It can be helpful to think about this as akin to four different people standing on four different corners of an intersection. All watch the same traffic move through the intersection, but each notices distinct aspects of what is taking place. Each field of study focuses on specific ways of knowing and viewing the world in which we live, and the people you will encounter in college classrooms take their disciplines very seriously—so seriously, in fact, that they have been immersed in formal academic study in their disciplines from three to ten years *after* college, not to mention any time they spent working in their respective fields.

Let's pretend, for example, that in your first semester of college you are taking a biology course, an art history course, an introductory philosophy course, and a course on Christianity at a Christian university. Now, although all of your professors are (probably) Christian and claim to follow Jesus, they will likely have different views of what is true.

The professor in your science course has been trained in the scientific method, which means she sees the world through a different lens than your religion professor. The science professor is going to approach any problem in life, after a bit of observation, to form a hypothesis about how it might be solved. Then she will set up an experiment of some sort to test her hypothesis. That experiment may or may not prove to be helpful in solving the problem. If it does, great! The issue is solved. If not, she will begin again with a new, more informed hypothesis. This professor, because of the training in her discipline, will value empirical and verifiable evidence. This means she wants to be able to observe what is taking place and, through an objective, experimental study, determine facts that will help to point to what appears to be true about the situation and problem she has encountered. So, in your biology course, the professor is going to talk about how the human body functions based on the mechanics of it—how the muscles, tendons, nerves, and brain impulses physically work together to move your limbs, keep your heart beating, and fill your lungs with oxygen.

The religion professor, on the other hand, sees the world through the eyes of faith and belief. He typically believes there is an interconnected nature between what is seen in the world around us and the unseen world of faith. A part of this person's daily life is to look on students and issues through eyes that see not only causes and effects but God's Spirit at work in and through circumstances, all in an effort for you to encounter the Jesus of the Bible and come to know and follow him as your own Lord and Savior. This person will be interested in issues of authority, justice, and what we choose to follow and look toward to inform us about what is important in life. While the science professor is interested in taking in the world through the senses, the religion professor is interested in seeing the world through eyes of faith. Additionally, the religion professor will be interested not only in observing the world as it is but also as it *ought* to be. This person will express a yearning to see people reconciled not only to God and each other but the whole of creation. It is these sorts of relationships that will provide meaning and purpose to life for the professor of religion.

See the difference? Neither is right or wrong; they are just different, and understanding this difference will go a long way toward helping us reconcile why a science class may approach questions about how old the earth is in a manner completely different from a religion class. These differences are not incompatible; in fact, they are equally important in helping us understand our world more completely. These two professors are different from the art and philosophy professors as well.

Your art history professor will likely see the world through symbols and with an eye on the form, composition, color, and effect a situation or encounter may have on a person. He is interested in the aesthetic of a situation and celebrates the beauty of the world and life as a mystery to be encountered. Art helps the artist express ideas, emotions, and situations that are inexpressible in words, so they turn to color, symbol, juxtaposition, and other techniques to communicate without words. This person is interested in issues of beauty and seeing beauty in all of life—even in the painful parts—as a way to embrace the human condition. It is not that he does not mourn tragedy but rather endeavors not to ignore the painful parts of life because they are just as true as the joyful parts. The art professor is not interested only in what is logical but also the imagination as well.

The philosophy professor is likely a person who is concerned with clarity, consistency, and thoughtfulness in communication and discussions. She is a person who deeply values logic, reason, accuracy, and enabling people to clarify what they mean and want to say so that others can properly and accurately understand. This professor is interested in examining the assumptions and presuppositions brought to discussions, in order to clarify starting points, in order to help people understand one another's point of view. Actually, philosophy is essentially the parent of all other disciplines because of its concern about these foundational issues. In other words, philosophy helps science, religion, and art to clarify, examine, and fine-tune their own understandings and arguments.

Clear as mud? What is important to take away from this section is that your different professors come from different points of view. This is due not only to their unique backgrounds and upbringings (which each of us embodies) but particularly to their academic training. Just keep in mind that these different disciplines view the world uniquely and that they do not conflict but rather help to create a more holistic understanding of what is true, beautiful, and good.

SYLLABUS

Your ally and *very* best help in understanding your professors' expectations and their course requirements are the syllabi they write for their courses. Many students do not realize that the syllabus serves as a quasi-legal document that functions like a contract. As with any contract, the professor outlines in the syllabus what is expected of a student, including policies about attendance, classroom etiquette, assignments, due dates, tests, quizzes, when class will meet, when it will not, etc., and, given how those expectations are fulfilled, the grades that students will receive. It does not have to be a mystery what exactly is expected of you. It is only necessary to carefully read the syllabus for all of this information. If, for some reason, something is not covered there, then that becomes a helpful and important question to raise in class. The professor will then see that you are a serious student, and the information gained will not only help you but your peers as well.

The details of the syllabus will reveal a great deal about your professor too. If it is precise in including every possible question a student could have, then you realize that you could have a very thorough professor who may not want to have to deal with many questions but would prefer to come to class and lecture without interruptions. On the other hand, if the syllabus leaves a lot of information unclear, it may reveal a professor who is flexible, or unorganized, or new. Figuring out which case applies to your specific professor is up to you. All professors are different, however, and learning them (not *about* them but learning *them*, as you would any other subject) will go far toward enabling you to earn the highest grade you can in their classes—and, more importantly, learn the material of the course.

A final thought regarding the syllabus: Keep it handy. Do not look at it once and then file it away (or throw it away), or you are bound to miss due dates and even entire assignments. Unlike high school, some professors will not even mention a paper or assignment that is due that week. They will simply assume you are aware of it since it is clearly outlined in the syllabus. So, instead of filing it away, study it regularly. I would even suggest writing down all due dates on your calendar (if you do not have a personal calendar, it is time to invest in one, whether paper or electronic), and you may find it helpful to go one step further by placing reminders a couple of weeks before the due dates for each assignment. These will serve as reminders to get started on whatever assignments are due, before they actually are.

ATTENDANCE

A vital piece of information that must be taken into account by every student is that of class attendance policies. In all likelihood, this will be clearly and prominently displayed in the syllabus. Unlike high school, it is unusual (even unheard of, except in serious situations) to have an excused absence in college. Each course will have a different attendance policy, depending on the professor, so pay attention. Generally speaking, there are not excused versus unexcused absences—there are only absences. So it is typical in a college course for there to be a stated number of acceptable missed classes for a student before it begins to affect his or her grade.

This information is crucial because losing points (or even failing a class) due to absences is about the most ridiculous way for you to ruin your hard work in a class and waste the money you paid to enroll in that course. Can you imagine reading all the class material, studying hard for all the tests and quizzes, investing hours writing research papers, all to earn a lower grade just because you blew off one (or came late to) too many classes? There is absolutely no reason for it. I cannot believe how many of my students earn lower grades due to this situation. Keep a close watch on how many times you have missed a class so that if you get sick or really need a break, you can take it without penalty. When in doubt, check with your professor.

During my freshman year, my roommate, Gustavo (Gus), developed a strange habit of not going to class at all. At some point during the first quarter, Gus discovered that he studied really well at night. The library was open late and even offered a 24-hour study room. He took full advantage of this. Gus simply found himself to be much more productive at night, so he essentially became nocturnal. His routine was to sleep all day (thus missing all his classes)—I often found him getting up as I returned to our room after track practice—get the homework and any class notes from friends, and then complete all the reading and assignments at night. This worked pretty well for him, except when it came to tests and quizzes administered in class. He kind of missed that detail and the fact that most professors expected students to regularly attend the class sessions. Gus failed all his classes that quarter and later was not allowed to return to the university for academic reasons. What a waste. Gus was smart enough to do well at the university level, but he was not a good enough student of his professors to understand the flaw in this plan.

Granted, this is a sort of extraordinary story, but it really happened, and you may be surprised to find how many sort of crazy ideas students can get in their heads during college—particularly during the freshman year. It is as if they believe they are the very first people to have ever had a particular idea or thought. If and when you ever get that idea (or your roommate does), remember what the wisest man who ever lived wrote in Ecclesiastes 1:9: "What has been will be again, what has been done will be done again; there is nothing new under the sun." If a thought is thought, it has likely been thought before. If an idea comes to you, it has likely come to someone else at some point. That is not to sound pessimistic but realistic and to say that going to college but not going to class is a bad idea. I just wish I had said that to Gus.

OFFICE HOURS

Another helpful piece of information you should find in the syllabus is your professors' office hours. These are the times that they are in their offices and welcome students to come by to ask questions about class, assignments, or perhaps even just to talk. Many professors are in their offices much more than during those hours, but being a college or university professor typically means that one is expected to be doing a lot more than simply teaching, advising, and grading. Most professors also do a fair amount of writing of articles, commentaries, books, and other such works. So, while they may physically be in their offices, it may not be appropriate to interrupt them. If it is an emergency, knock and make it quick. If it is not an emergency, send an email or ask in class.

A piece of advice I will suggest to all students but particularly for those who may be attending large universities and in classes of one hundred or more (or hundreds) of students, be sure to visit each of your professors during their office hours at least one time during the term. It is an opportunity for you to have short conversations with them one on one; it can be a perfect opportunity to pay them some form of compliment for something they have helped you learn; and it will give them a face to go with your name. This can be particularly helpful for you if your grade ends up being on the border between, say, a B or a C. Sometimes it comes down to a point or two. A personal visit with a professor may help influence that grade in your favor. It may not as well, but a personal visit during office hours will not likely be anything but good for you and your professor too.

CLASSROOM ETIQUETTE

A third essential point to be gathered from the syllabus is what a professor deems appropriate classroom behavior. Things that fall into this category are issues like bringing food to class, using a computer or texting while in class, and many other miscellaneous items. It could be that a particular professor may not want hats to be worn in class. Another may abhor students who fall asleep in class. These sorts of common and uncommon issues may be addressed on the syllabus and are very important.

A couple of personal pet peeves of mine are computers and cell phones in class. The university at which I teach is a wireless campus, so you can find an open internet signal all over campus, including classrooms. Students who have wireless internet access on their laptops or phones can access that signal during class. Some use it to Google something we are talking about, which can be helpful, but others use it to update their Facebook statuses, which is not particularly helpful (especially when their statuses are "bored in Kipp's class"). As a result, I have banned computers from my classes. If you pull one out during one of my classes, you will be marked absent for the day (same applies if you text in class). *Big deal, one absence*—you may think. But after four absences in one of my classes, students lose 40 points. After five absences, they lose 100. Typically 100 points is an entire grade point—meaning, although you may have earned a B, you just got a C. That is a big deal. The moral: Be sure to know and follow the syllabus guidelines for classroom etiquette.

LATE ASSIGNMENTS

A fourth important point to learn from the syllabus is the late-work policy. As you can imagine, if you turn in an assignment or paper late, you will end up losing points even before the first word of your masterpiece is read. The reality here is that you want to do all you possibly can to turn in all your work on time. That means to note due dates in your phone or computer or, if you're old school, write them on your calendar. Turning in work late is another really silly way to lower your grade. With a little planning, it is completely unnecessary. Frankly, an adequately written paper turned in on time will often earn a better grade than a well-written paper turned in late. The reason for this is that a late paper is read at a different time from all the other papers, and that often means it is looked at more closely and, at times, critically; so it pays to get it in on time.

However, life happens, sometimes all in the same week, meaning that your computer crashes, you get sick, and your best friend breaks up with her boyfriend and needs *you.* These things happen, and usually the week you have three big papers due. When a week like this hits you (and believe me, it is a *when* and not an *if*), then you need to know which professor has the most lenient late policy because, if you're like many college students, you were planning on writing all of these papers the week they were due. (Not to be a buzz kill, but do try not to leave all your papers to write the week before they are due. Get started earlier and have time to proofread. Your papers will be better. Your grades will be better. Your professors will like you more.) If you find yourself in a situation like this and realize there is no way for you to write three excellent papers in the fifteen hours you have before they are all due, then you will need to prioritize. For example, knowing that you are going to lose 50 percent if a paper is late in one class versus only 10 percent in another and perhaps no penalty in your third class is helpful and means that you better put all your mental and physical energy into writing the paper for the first class. Once it is done, you can work on the second paper. I would leave the third paper for the next day after you sleep some, if there is no penalty for being late.

Regardless of whether you think a situation like this is going to happen to you, you *do* need to know what turning in assignments late means to your grade.

ONLINE COURSES

All that has been written about the syllabus applies to both a traditional class as well as an online one with one exception. In an online course, you generally do not have class time to seek clarity about anything that is unclear in the syllabus. For this reason, it is extremely important for professors to be crystal clear in the syllabi of online courses. When this does not happen, the onus is on you—the student—to seek that clarity.

As someone who has taken online courses and now teaches them, let me share a few thoughts about them. First, the number of online course offerings is absolutely exploding in comparison to traditional course offerings. What this means is that you will likely encounter the opportunity or even necessity of taking an online course at some point in your college career. All online courses are not created equally, however. For an online course to be of a sufficient quality that it is worth your time and effort, three things need to take place in it.

First there needs to be a high amount of interaction between the professor and you, the student. This means the professor is involved in the online discussion (often involving a discussion board or some way to interact in an asynchronous manner). If the professor is not logging in several times each week, this may not be the kind of course you want to spend your tuition dollars on.

Second, a quality online course stimulates a high amount of interaction between the pupil and the content.

This is to say that you are reading texts, listening to lectures, viewing short film clips, etc., and must actively be involved as a student in this course. This is the part of online courses that is most easily facilitated by the instructor because this simply means they assign reading or other ways to get you to interact with the content.

The last trait of a quality online course is that there is a high level of interaction between students. This means that students have to talk to each other online. One of the ways that this may take place is through a discussion board where students are assigned to post their reactions to or thoughts about something they read or interacted with and then to read and respond to the other students' thoughts. This is the way class discussion takes place in an online course. Like the interaction with the instructor, this probably ought to happen several times a week to be legitimate.

It is important to note that this part of an online course can actually be better than a face-to-face course. Think about it. In a face-to-face course, some students may never say a word in class. They essentially hide in plain sight by never speaking. In an online environment, this is not possible if student interaction is required. And what we know from research is that the learning that takes place through interaction with peers is just as valuable as the learning that takes place by listening to the professor or reading the text. This is really important to consider when thinking about taking an online course.

FINDING A RHYTHM FOR YOUR LIFE

There is a time for *everything*, and a season
for *every activity* under the heavens: a time
to be born and a time to die, a time to plant
and a time to uproot, a time to kill and a time
to heal, a time to tear down and a time to
build, a time to weep and a time to laugh, a
time to mourn and a time to dance, a time to
scatter stones and a time to gather them, a
time to embrace and a time to refrain from
embracing, a time to search and a time to
give up, a time to keep and a time to throw
away, a time to tear and a time to mend, a
time to be silent and a time to speak, a time
to love and a time to hate, a time for war and
a time for peace. What do workers gain from
their toil? I have seen the burden God has laid
on the human race. He has made everything
beautiful in its time. He has also set eternity
in the human heart; yet no one can fathom
what God has done from beginning to end. I
know that there is nothing better for people
than to be happy and to do good while they

live. That each of them may eat and drink, and *find satisfaction in all their toil*—this is the gift of God.

—Ecclesiastes 3:1-13, emphasis added

When I'm overwhelmed with things to do, I like to remember this passage from Ecclesiastes. Ecclesiastes is a part of the biblical literature known as wisdom literature. This literature is respected for its astute common sense and, at times, deep insight into the human condition. The wisdom gleaned in this particular passage is that there is a time for everything and a season for all the things that need to be accomplished. The season of college is a season for study and getting things done. Knowing this and that college does not last but a few precious years can help stem some of the feelings of being overwhelmed. It will not always be like this. In fact, each semester comes to an end, and that end signals a cessation of homework.

Being a student is unlike any other part of life, where there are often no breaks from one's labor (or toil, as Ecclesiastes calls it). Because, when you get your first job, it does not matter if you are on vacation, having your first child, or healing from a significant injury, deadlines are deadlines, and they can come at any time. In fact, the boundary lines of college (with the beginning and end of each semester) are a wonderful false reality separate from the rest of life.

As a creature of habit, I find that I do better and even feel better about life when I have a routine and plan for my day. A plan helps me purposefully move into and through my day with an idea of what is to be accomplished. I have found that without a plan I can be easily distracted by whatever comes up.

With the multitude of distractions that can be found on any college campus, a student is going to end up never studying without a plan to do so—and I encourage you to plan to do so regularly. The point I'm trying to make is that at college you will have time to play, and you need to, but you have got to plan to study, or the play will quickly take over your life. With intramural sports, clubs, organizations, important causes, dorm parties, service opportunities, fundraisers, campus-wide emphases, and a host of other things taking place, a student without a time-management plan will soon be an overcommitted student. That over commitment may be to good things, but if they are not the right things, they can be distractions from the primary purpose of going to college—an education and, ultimately, a degree.

It is common for new freshmen to over commit. I have seen it time and time again. Freshmen are enthusiastic, magnetic people, and others are drawn to them, to such a degree that everyone wants them to be a part of their cause. This means lots of invitations to be involved in lots of organizations, which can be a wonderful boost to one's self esteem. However, without the ability to say no, you can quickly find yourself having said yes to too many things and becoming frustrated. Part of the answer is to create a schedule that allows ample time for play and study, and when the meetings or requests cannot fit into that schedule, decline—for now. Next semester may be a different story, but do not over commit, or you will find yourself letting down the very people and causes you were so passionate about.

SCHEDULE

Many students find it helpful to establish a regular weekly plan. Typically, that plan is anchored by class times and any meetings that might occur weekly. Once these non-negotiable and primary engagements are on your calendar, then you can fit in the other, secondary activities. One of the first secondary activities (secondary only because it does not have a scheduled meeting time like a class) I would encourage you to place on your calendar is study time. If you plan a minimum of two hours per day Monday through Friday and then are disciplined enough to stick to them, you will find that you can accomplish quite a lot—perhaps most of what you need—during your week. What can be really helpful about this sort of plan is that it does not leave all your homework until the weekend when you might like to do other things besides just studying. In all reality, you will probably still spend a good portion of time on Saturday afternoons in the library or with some study groups, but being disciplined to use your week will significantly lighten your load on the weekends. And who *doesn't* want to have less homework on the weekend?

Of course, it is also important to schedule time for other meaningful activities, like exercise, hanging out with good friends, extracurricular activities, and even just some scheduled time to do nothing—really. You may find your life so filled with activity during college that to plan to have an hour or two each week to do nothing can be quite refreshing.

As a rule of thumb, you might consider splitting up your waking hours in some manner like 40 percent academic (classes and study); 40 percent social (friends, activities, meals, etc.); and 20 percent other (exercise, relaxation, hanging out, flex time that can be used as needed).

SLEEP

An *extremely* important part of remaining healthy during the college experience—and often a terribly disrespected reality by college students—is planning adequate down time. This is time that may seem negotiable since you are young and energetic but, if neglected, will mean sickness, burnout, or worse.

Dorm life can certainly challenge getting to bed early, but that does not mean you cannot still get enough sleep. As an athlete during high school and college, I realized I needed rest. At home I was typically in bed by 11:00 and then up around 6:30. Although 7.5 hours was probably not what I ought to have had it was okay and better than many of my peers. In the freshman dorm, however, this radically changed. The dorms operated at a volume level of about 7 or 8, on a scale of 10, until around 1:00 or 2:00 a.m.; then it came down to a 5. It was not quiet, not by a long shot, but with the aid of earplugs, I was able to get to sleep most nights by 1:00 or 2:00 a.m. That was pretty late for me, which was okay unless I had an 8:00 a.m. class. The moral of this story: Do your very best to schedule classes no earlier than 9:00 a.m. (or later if possible) because that extra hour or so of sleep will make a big difference.

I can't remember where I heard it, but a few years back, after being plagued with a series of flu-like symptoms, I heard that one of the biggest things a person could do to ward off sickness was get plenty of sleep. My brother tells me that he is fine with four or five hours a night, but I have to be honest and say that I am an eight-to-nine-hour-a-night guy! Eight hours is sometimes pushing it for me, and as my alarm screams, I wake up groggy and grumpy from a dead sleep! Before having kids, I might have gotten a bout of the flu about once a year, but once those babies started to interact with other kids, our home was like a Petri dish! Runny noses and toddlers who hadn't learned how to cover their mouths when they sneezed. So when I heard this advice of getting enough rest, I really took it to heart, and from that point on, I've been on an 8½-to-9-hours-a-night regime. And let me tell you, it has made all the difference. I am now an official sleep convert!

But back in college, it was the cool thing to do all sorts of crazy things in the wee hours of the night. Just having the option to stay up as late as I wanted to, chatting with my roommate, gave me such a sense of freedom. And during finals week, you could find the waitresses at the local diner, Farm

Boy, pouring coffee into the mugs of college students 'til all hours of the night. TA's burrito shop did some of their best business after 11:00 p.m. So I understand the challenge.

It's probably been a long time since you had an enforced bedtime. But let's look at the data that tells us getting enough sleep is a big deal. According to the Harvard Health Publications, published by Harvard Medical School, sleep affects many aspects of our lives, including mood, learning and memory, immune function, and weight gain. I've already testified about the immune function aspect. As far as mood goes, when people lose sleep, they can become irritable, impatient, and have a difficult time concentrating.[15] Entering college can be an exciting time of meeting different people and learning new things, but living away from home for the first time can also be emotional, and certainly you do not need something as simple as sleep to exasperate the situation. You need to be at your best to absorb all the new stimuli of the campus, friends, and activities.

As well as being in a good mood, "sleep helps the brain commit new information to memory through a process called memory consolidation."[16] Get your hours in, and you'll do better on tests! According to the Mayo Clinic, individuals who get little sleep over several nights do not perform well on complex mental tasks, yet those who get closer to seven

15. "Importance of Sleep: 6 Reasons Not to Scrimp on Sleep." *Harvard Health Publications,* Harvard Medical School, Jan. 2006. Web. 14 January 2011.

16. Ibid.

hours of sleep have better performance. For adults (that's you!) consider seven to nine hours a night as a guideline.[17]

Agreeing with this concept of adequate sleep may not be your challenge; trying to find a quiet place to get the sleep might be more the issue. So consider these few suggestions, and be creative enough to find some solutions of your own. If your roommate is amicable, set some agreed-upon guidelines for quiet time in the evenings and where you might go if one of you decides you are not ready to go to bed. Also consider finding some empty-nest surrogate parents in your college town who have a spare bedroom they may be willing to let you use once in a while. If they do still have kids at home, maybe you can strike a bargain of trading babysitting for a home away from home. And, if all else fails, I took some pretty serious naps on the top floor of my college campus's library. Again, be creative!

"The American Academy of Sleep Medicine (AASM) offers the following tips on how to get a good night's sleep:

- Follow a consistent bedtime routine.

- Establish a relaxing setting at bedtime.

- Get a full night's sleep every night.

- Avoid foods or drinks that contain caffeine, as well as any medicine that has a stimulant, prior to bedtime.

- Do not stay up all hours of the night to cram for an exam, do homework, etc. If after-school activities are

17. Morgenthaler, Timothy. "How Many Hours of Sleep Are Enough for Good Health?" Mayo Clinic, 4 December 2010. Web. 15 January 2011.

proving to be too time-consuming, consider cutting back on these activities.

- Do not go to bed hungry, but don't eat a big meal before bedtime either.
- Avoid any rigorous exercise within six hours of your bedtime.
- Make your bedroom quiet, dark and a little bit cool.
- Get up at the same time every morning."[18]

SABBATH AND REST

I have always attempted to do all I can to live in harmony with Scripture and the teachings of the church. One commandment I struggled to follow all through college, however, was the fourth: "Observe the Sabbath day by keeping it holy as the Lord your God has commanded you. Six days you shall labor and do all your work, but the seventh day is a Sabbath to the Lord your God. On it you shall not do any work" (Deuteronomy 5: 12-14). What does it mean to be a Christian college student and observe this commandment? Are a student's homework, studies, and paper writing work? How can a student possibly *not* study on Sunday?

As a student who was a serious Christian but not attending a Christian college, I often found myself studying on Sundays. My routine was to attend church in the morning,

18. About.com. *http://youngadults.about.com/gi/o.htm?zi=1/XJ&zTi=1&sdn=youngadults&cdn=parenting&tm=7&f=20&tt=2&bt=1&bts=0&st=15&zu=http%3A//www.aasmnet.org/Articles.aspx%3Fid%3D887* (accessed December 30, 2010)

eat lunch with friends after church, then hit the library for the rest of the afternoon. There were times I struggled with this seeming contradiction, yet I did not know how to accomplish what needed to be done any other way.

As a seminary student, I struggled even more. I felt even more convicted—not so much about studying on Sundays (since, for a pastor, Sunday is a workday) but about never taking a day off. It seemed beyond question that God intended for us to have a day off of work. That's why Genesis, in describing God's good creation, takes time to point out that God ceases from activity to rest. I became convinced that I had no right to always work. After all, who am I not to take a rest when even God did?

I got around all of this as a youth pastor by taking a day off during the week. But as a student who also had a nearly full-time job at a church, this was difficult. I experimented with various things but continued to struggle and not find a great solution.

Finally, as a doctoral student and full-time faculty member, I realized I *had* to honor this command because I believed I was suffering, as was my relationship with God, due to my disobedience. So I simply committed to not doing homework on Sunday. Instead of homework, I read some things I *wanted* to read—a crazy concept for a doctoral student. I napped, I took a walk with my family, I played games with my kids, and I called my out-of-state family members. It was incredible. That next week I was all the more determined to get done what needed to be done between Monday and Saturday. And I did it.

I found that what was required was not complicated but rather a simple and determined commitment to honor what God commanded. And when I did so, it seemed my six days were more than adequate to complete what was needed.

NUTRITION

Whether your mother made you eat your veggies and sent you outside for some fresh air each day, now is your chance to decide some life essentials on your own. Awaiting your arrival at college are all types of choices to be made, and some may sound trivial but actually may determine if you simply survive college or thrive! What enters your body, your daily R&R, and the amount you move will influence significantly your mood, energy level, and even how many days you spend in bed with the flu. So if your mom never taught you these basics, listen up now!

Let's start with food. This may sound a bit boring, but here's the deal. Some foods are your friends, and others are not. There are ones that may seem the friendliest and most inviting, but beware, all they do is fill an empty void (your belly), which is not enough to sustain your amazing body for very long. You see, what your body does is take the food and process all it contains, so food packed with lots of nutrients (vitamins, minerals, and other micronutrients) will not only fill the void, it will give you sustaining energy, brain power, defense against sickness, and assist in mainte-nance—building and rebuilding your body, from the cellular level all the way up to bones and skin.

Let's be honest. It is no secret that many of those headed for college are also headed for the "freshman fifteen." If you have never heard this phrase, it refers to the number of pounds students gain in their first year of college. Whether that is really the true average, typically most college students gain weight. According to *USA Today,* "60% of students said they gained weight from the beginning of their freshman year to the beginning of their sophomore year. The women said they put on 7.5 pounds; men, almost 9."[19]

It is difficult not to consider all the options available on a daily basis from the campus cafeteria. At my school, the options were endless—the fried food, the sandwich bar, soft-serve ice cream, salad bar, hot entrées, cookies galore, etc. All you can and ever wanted to eat, three times a day! Of course, not all meal plans are the same, and depending on how big your school is, there may be a variety of plans to choose from. There may be an option for you to just have two meals per day, and that leaves some flexibility for you to create your own dining experience out of your dorm room or apartment. Then the choices become a little wider; what will you decide to buy from the grocery store to stock your mini fridge or what kind of take-out you will purchase from the nearest restaurants.

Practically speaking, if you are trying to figure out which foods are packed with the most good stuff, consider these guidelines: pulled from the ground, picked from a tree, or

---

19. Hellmich, Nancy. "Beer, Bad Habits Fuel College Weight Gain. *USA Today,* 28 October 2008. Web. 13 January 2011.

used to walk or swim around. And, generally speaking, food that has been packaged, processed, or otherwise manipulated will have less power to its punch. The less processing, the better the food. Take bread, for instance. There is whole-wheat bread, which takes the wheat kernel, grinds it up, adds yeast, water, and maybe a little sweetener, and you have a wholesome product containing tons of natural-made nutrients and fiber. On the flip side, white bread (often called wheat bread but, mind you, not whole-wheat bread), takes that once whole wheat kernel, strips off the bran (outer layer containing fiber and essential-for-you minerals like iron), the germ (the seed inside the kernel that grows into a wheat plant and is rich in many vitamins and minerals to support new life), and leaves us with the endosperm (a starchy, low-protein, vitamin- and mineral-deficient part of the kernel).[20] Mix that with yeast, water and sweetener, and you basically have filler but not a builder. After a while, fillers are just not enough, and your body begins to suffer. Interestingly enough, our government has determined white bread to be *so* deficient in essential nutrients that, in order to prevent widespread chronic disease from occurring in our country, it requires that all grain products crossing state lines add back four synthetically produced vitamins along with iron, out of the eleven natural vitamins and sixteen minerals that were removed—thus the *enriched* label on white and non-whole-wheat breads.[21]

20. Ellie Whitney, Rolfes, S. Rady. *Understanding Nutrition*, eleventh edition. Thomas Higher Education, Belmont, CA, 2008. 52-53.

21. Carter, J. Stein. *Vitamins*. University of Cincinnati Clermont College, 2 November 2004. Web. 14 January 2011.

Now that you know on a basic level how to identify the good-for-you food, if you want to keep healthy from a nutrition perspective, just follow this one easy and simple guideline: For each meal, make sure that half your food is fruit and/or vegetables. What does that look like? Possibly, a sandwich with a portion of carrot sticks, fruit, and salad equal to the size of the sandwich. Or a bowl of cereal with fresh fruit on the side. A plate half full of the daily entrée (such as some meat and rice, or meat lasagna) and the other half of the plate full of vegetables or salad. *Focus on what you need to eat (fruits, vegetables, whole grains, etc.), as opposed to what you should not eat, so that you will be spending more of your mental energy trying to get it all in as opposed to depriving yourself.* Does that make sense? It's all in how you look at it.

Your daily intake of vegetables should be 2 ½ to 3 cups, and fruit intake should be about 2 cups. That's quite a bit! Knowing that information helps me decide midafternoon that if I'm going to get my fruit and veggie allowance in for the day, I'd better choose an apple over a cookie! Of course, you do need other food groups in your diet, so don't neglect your dairy, meat, and grains. Those groups will be on the non-produce side of your plate.

EXERCISE

Adjusting to college takes enough time in itself, so sometimes it's easy to forget about incorporating physical activity into your schedule. Back at home, I was used to the gym membership we had as a family so that when I got to college, it was rather a surprise how much out-of-pocket expense I would have to sacrifice to get my weekly aerobics classes in (yes, this was back in the '80s!). After draining my bank account on various expenditures, I was left without any options except getting out to the track for a run, but I was *not* a runner! It took sheer desperation (the need to exercise plus a lack of money) to realize that running and walking are truly some of the best activities, simply because all you need are shoes!

If you venture outside for your exercise, you not only get fresh air but some Vitamin D. I recommend running and walking because they are easy and cheap, and you can do it most anywhere. Fortunately, most college campuses have gyms with various equipment available to all students. Classes are another option, and some are designed to be for credit and others simply for recreation. It's a good idea to look into these resources early in your first term so you can take advantage of all that your tuition enables you to do.

I imagine some of you are not too familiar with this exercise and running topic. But it's important that you listen up. If to date you have been something of a couch potato, for many reasons it's time to get up, get out, and breathe some fresh air. Your mood will be brighter, your appetite lighter, and your energy higher. Whether you struggle with keeping your weight down, exercise is a vital part of living a vibrant and healthy life. Our current lifestyle—with computers to work, video games to play, cars to take us where we need to go, and garage door openers to ensure that we never need to step too far—is a recipe for a sedentary existence.

The U.S. Department of Health and Human Services published its first ever Physical Activity Guideline in 2008. Inactivity among Americans is high, and doing physical activity is one of the most important ways of retaining good health. "These guidelines are necessary because of the importance of physical activity to the health of Americans, whose current inactivity puts them at unnecessary risk."[22] Centers for Disease Control and Prevention tells us that each week we should be engaging in muscle-strengthening activity one or more days (rock climbing, anyone?), and one hour and fifteen minutes of vigorous-intensity activity, or two and a half hours of moderate-intensity activity.[23] But remember, if you are at zero now, *anything* is an improvement. For goodness' sake, even parking at the far side of the parking lot is helpful! And take the stairs instead of the elevator. Incorporating simple habits into your life can and will make all the difference.

I hope it makes sense to you by this point to take care of yourself. You have been beautifully made by an amazing Creator. Take care of his amazing work, *made in his own image*. And consider this: "For you created my inmost be-

22. *Physical Activity Guidelines for Americans*. Office of Disease Prevention & Health Promotion (*http://odphp.osophs.dhhs.gov/*), U.S. Department of Health and Human Services (*http://www.hhs.gov/*). 21 November 2008. Web. 15 January 2011.

23. *How Much Physical Activity Do Adults Need?* Centers for Disease Control and Prevention. 10 May 2010. Web. 15 January 2011.

ing; you knit me together in my mother's womb. I praise you because *I am fearfully and wonderfully made*; your works are wonderful, I know that full well" (Psalm 139 13-14, emphasis added).

HYGIENE

What a fun section title! I bet you are just riveted to the page. Seriously, though, living in most college dorms is *not* like living at home. Unless you are fortunate enough to have a private shower in your room, suite, pod, or whatever it's called at your institution, you are not really in control of the cleanliness of your bathing facilities. (This may actually be quite good news for some of you who have not yet learned the sacred art of toilet cleaning and shower scale removal.)

The point here is that, unlike when you lived at home, wearing flip flops in the community bathroom is highly recommended. Know what plantar warts are? They are a stubborn, living thing that can begin growing on the bottom of your foot. How do you engage one of these things and invite them to live with you? Simply by being barefoot in public places where folks with plantar warts have walked. Want one? Just walk barefoot in your community showers (and, depending upon the number of roommates you have in your room, suite, or pod, that bathroom may qualify as community too); sooner or later, you'll end up with one or more.

Actually, to be honest, some really strong and dangerous bacteria and disease can end up in places where a lot of people shower or sweat. There is something really life giving for some bacteria in warm, moist places like locker rooms, bathrooms, and workout facilities. If you pay attention to the news much, you've probably heard random stories of athletes and even just ordinary college students contracting some serious stuff through contact with public bathrooms, wrestling mats, and even just from *sitting* on public exercise equipment.

You know those cleaning supplies that are provided to wipe down the elliptical machine or stationary bike at your school's gym facility? They actually can make the difference between you contracting a serious disease and not. I strongly encourage you to use them before *and* after you use public exercise equipment (unless, of course, you are certain it has already been wiped down thoroughly). The before obviously is for you; the after is for the next person.

Hopefully you'll never even have an opportunity to contract some of the more serious bacteria for meningitis, MRSA, or some other unpleasant, life-sucking equivalent, but even avoiding the flu or other more common maladies makes taking an extra fifteen seconds to wipe down a surface or throw on some flip flops well worth it.

PART 4: GOING BACK HOME

Max Lucado tells this story in his book *No Wonder They Call Him Savior*:

The small house was simple but adequate. It consisted of one large room on a dusty street. Its red-tiled roof was one of many in this poor neighborhood on the outskirts of the Brazilian village. It was a comfortable home. Maria and her daughter, Christina, had done what they could to add color to the gray walls and warmth to the hard dirt floor an old calendar, a faded photograph of a relative, a wooden crucifix. The furnishings were modest: a pallet on either side of the room, a washbasin, and a wood-burning stove.

Maria's husband had died when Christina was an infant. The young mother, stubbornly refusing opportunities to remarry, got a job and set out to raise her young daughter. And now, fifteen years later, the worst years were over. Though Maria's salary as a maid afforded few luxuries, it was reliable, and it did provide food and clothes. And now, Christina was old enough to get a job to help out.

Some said Christina got her independence from her mother. She recoiled at the traditional idea of marrying young and raising a family. Not that she couldn't have had her pick of husbands. Her olive skin and brown eyes kept a steady stream of prospects at her door. She had an infectious way of throwing her head back and filling the room with laughter. She also had that rare magic some women have that makes every man feel like a king just by being near them. But it was her spirited curiosity that made her keep all the men at arm's length.

She spoke often of going to the city. She dreamed of trading her dusty neighborhood for exciting avenues and city life. Just the thought of this horrified her mother. Maria was always quick to remind Christina of the harshness of the streets.

"People don't know you there. Jobs are scarce, and the life is cruel. And besides, if you went there, what would you do for a living?"

Maria knew exactly what Christina would have to do for a living. That's why her heart broke when she awoke one morning to find her daughter's bed empty. Maria knew immediately where her daughter had gone. She also knew immediately what she must do to find her. She quickly threw some clothes in a bag, gathered up all her money, and ran out of the house.

On her way to the bus stop, she entered a drugstore to get one last thing. Pictures. She sat in the photograph booth, closed the curtain, and spent all she could on pictures of herself. With her purse full of small black and white photos, she boarded the next bus to Rio de Janeiro.

Maria knew Christina had no way of earning money. She also knew that her daughter was too stubborn to give up. When pride meets hunger, a human will do things that were before unthinkable. Knowing this,

Maria began her search. Bars, hotels, nightclubs, any place with a reputation for streetwalkers or prostitutes. She went to them all. And at each place she left her picture—taped to a hotel bulletin board, fastened to a corner phone booth. And on the back of each photo, she wrote a note.

It wasn't too long before both the money and the pictures ran out, and Maria had to go home. The weary mother wept as the bus began its long journey back to her small village.

It was a few weeks later that young Christina descended the hotel stairs. Her face was tired. Her brown eyes no longer danced with youth but spoke of pain and fear. Her laughter was broken. Her dream had become a nightmare. A thousand times over she had longed to trade these countless beds for her secure pallet. Yet the little village was, in too many ways, too far away.

As she reached the bottom of the stairs, her eyes noticed a familiar face. She looked again, and there on the lobby mirror was a small picture of her mother. Christina's eyes burned, and her throat tightened as she walked across the room and removed the small photo. Written on the back was this compelling invitation: *Whatever you have done, whatever you have become, it doesn't matter. Please come home.*

She did.[24]

---

24. Lucado, Max. *No Wonder They Call Him Savior.* Thomas Nelson. Nashville, TN. 1986.

Going home can be wonderful: memories of childhood, the familiar smells and feelings, and all the emotions that have been experienced in that place. It can also be difficult: memories of childhood, the familiar smells and feelings, and all the emotions that have been experienced in that place. It depends a lot on the home, the people who live there, the person returning, and the relationships shared between all of these. A lot can happen in a person's life in a relatively short time. Christina certainly experienced that. Although she was only gone a month or two, she ended up doing things she never planned to do and becoming someone she never planned to become. In fact, you might say she was a completely different person than when she left. Going to college is a *very* different kind of experience than the one Christina had, but it is important not to dismiss the two as having nothing in common. There are some definite similarities.

When Christina left her sleepy village for the city, she had big plans. She was excited to live life and experience the adventure and night life of a bustling place like Rio. Of course, she did not plan on the tragic turn her life took; she only dreamed of success and fun and discovery. What happened was very different, but it certainly was not her intent, starting out, to make the kind of choices she did.

Similarly unfortunately, the dreams of every freshman setting off for college do not always end up coming true. In fact, there are times that things can end up going wrong, and once idealistic and excited freshmen can crash and burn. It is then that one hopes that home is a welcoming place that will accept them back to heal and recover. Of course, the majority of freshmen have a fantastic experience their first semesters. It is important that you plan ahead to *make* this happen and not just *hope* it does.

By now, you are well acquainted with my own college journey. Something I have not mentioned was how my freshman year was sort of a crash-and-burn experience. I will spare you all the minutiae, but suffice it to say that when spring break came around that year, I was probably *too* excited to leave campus for a week. I was so excited, in fact, that I never really made it back to school. Technically, I *physically* returned, but my heart and focus did not. Just two days into that last term before summer break, I made the radical (at least for me) decision to quit school.

Once this was decided, I acted so quickly that I was officially withdrawn from the university, checked out of my dorm, packed, and on my way home before I thought to call my parents. When I did, I didn't exactly tell them what was happening, at least not at first. I was actually driving home and had already left the town in which my school was located when I stopped to make a call on a pay phone (yeah—I'm old). It was almost an afterthought, but I thought it was perhaps a good idea not to just show up on my parents' doorstep.

Since I was the youngest of four and the first to go away to college right out of high school, I think my parents hoped my college journey would be a bit more direct from start to graduation. My oldest two siblings did not go to college, and the brother closest to me in age was slowly working his way through college (it took him nine years in all) while he worked full time. There is absolutely nothing wrong with the paths each of them took, but since my dad was an educator and had earned his doctorate (while working full time with a wife and four kids), I think he expected his kids to attend college.

When I made that call, my dad answered. I explained to him that I thought I was going to quit school (not exactly the truth, since I already had). He immediately disagreed with that decision and strongly advised me to stay the course and complete the year. When I 'fessed up to the reality that I had already left, I asked him if I could come home. I'll never forget his response: "Mike, you can always come home." That caused an emotional landslide of relief. I had not really considered the possibility that maybe my folks would not allow me to return. As I was making that phone call, I suddenly realized the assumptions I had made, and I was very nervous.

Although he *strongly* disagreed with the decision I had made, he welcomed me home. I glimpsed in that moment some of what the prodigal son (see Luke 15: 11-32 for the story in its entirety) must have felt when he was welcomed home by his gracious father. Although I had not "squandered my inheritance on wild living" (in fact, I had paid my way that entire first two terms of college), I was now making my own decision that was not in sync with my parents' hopes and dreams for my life. That was difficult for all of us but an important step in my growth toward adulthood. (The rest of the story: I was back in school that next fall at our community college and even got caught up on credits by taking 21 and 22 credits each semester. Although that was not necessary or even advisable, it is what I did.)

CHRISTMAS BREAK

I really enjoy hearing about the things my students did during their Christmas break, so typically, on the first day back in the classroom, before getting involved in class material, I ask some of them to share their stories with the class. Some share unbelievable tales of travel (sometimes involving vehicle-breakdown adventures) and fun; others express that things were pretty much as expected; and some are just glad to be back at school because they were so bored to be home.

Something I have learned, however, is that if I dig down a little below the surface, an experience that is nearly universal to new freshmen is the sense of personal growth and change they recognize as they return home. Although it has only been four months and everyone at home is basically the same, they have changed quite a bit.

One recent Christmas, I received this poem that is a great illustration of exactly this concept. It was written by a male freshman who came to our university as a true freshman (not having attended college before) but who is a bit older than the norm. He gave his permission to include it here in hopes that it may be helpful to someone else.

I left my home
To follow the dream of a young boy
To follow the call on a boy's heart

I left my home
Filled with guilt for leaving
Filled with shame for waiting too long

I left my home
Searching for purpose because I was lost
Searching for God because I couldn't find him

I came back home
A man who left his childhood behind him
A man struggling with a call he cannot deny

I came back home
To find life moved on without me
To find I am no longer needed where I once was

I came back home
Too afraid to become the man I must
Too afraid of what God might ask of me

I leave my family
My friends behind
With their love always with me
I cannot help but wonder
If I should I come back again
I fear I may soon be asked
To continue with only God by my side
And I'm afraid when the time comes
I won't have the strength to say, "Yes Lord"

I left my home

Must I leave my past as well?

—Kenneth

What strikes me most about Kenneth's poem is the sense that *he* has changed. "I came back home a man who has left his childhood behind him." What a powerful expression of the personal growth and change he experienced over the course of four months. That is what college is supposed to be about. But I sense a tone of reticence as well as excitement in his poem. Although there is an implied excitement about the growth, there is also a grief. Often change is experienced as loss because we are no longer who we once were. This is not a bad thing; in fact, in terms of personal growth and maturity, it is quite good, but that does not mean it is easy.

My first Christmas back home proved to be a confusing time. I loved being with my parents and family, giving them each sweatshirts purchased in my school's bookstore, and sleeping in my own bed. It was wonderful. The confusing part came in negotiating my relationship with my parents and particularly my old friends who stayed at home instead of attending college. My parents were great. They had been treating me as a young adult before I left for college, so that relationship just continued, but I was confused by that. I mean, I was 18 and an "adult," but I still didn't feel like one.

The new status of college student just added to my sense of not quite knowing what I was—adult or child. After all, now I was living away from home, I had made it through my first term at college, and I had experienced a significant amount of maturity…but still slept in the same bed in the room I had occupied since ninth grade. The fact of the matter was that I was neither child nor adult. I was an emerging adult (discussed back in Part 2) and needed only to *choose* to accept the lack of clarity of this period of life and enjoy the ride.

Most difficult to negotiate were the relationships with friends who stayed home or attended the local community college. For the record, there is absolutely nothing wrong with going to a community college (I went to two), and in fact, it is for some the best route to take. The confusion caused by these relationships was more about how much I had experienced and changed (grown up) and my own perception that these old friends had not. That is not to say in an absolute sense whether they had or had not grown or changed but rather my own personal *perception*. It is said that "perception is greater than fact," meaning that regardless of what the truth might be, a person's perception of what is true is what counts functionally. And my perception was that I had experienced all of these changes, choices, new relationships, etc., and they had not. Like Kenneth expresses in his poem, there was a sense that I had left "my family and friends behind" and was in a new place. That can create a sense of loneliness and isolation.

This was where the confusion entered. After four long months of being separate, I was *physically* with the people I had missed so much—family members and old friends— and yet I felt separate from them. Crazy, isn't it? The relationships with friends who had gone away to other colleges and universities were much less confusing. We had much to talk about. We compared our different experiences of dorm life, cafeteria food, new professors, campus life, and even the churches we had visited. These friends and I seemed better able to connect. We perceived similar changes in each other that we did not perceive in the friends that did not go away to school.

I'm sure this is not the experience of every freshman who goes home, but it was mine and seems to be more common than not as I speak to freshmen each year about their Christmas breaks. What is important about this experience is to expect it. It will not necessarily make it easier, but it will help not to be surprised by it. Each of us has to encounter these situations on our own terms, but realizing they are coming can be helpful for everyone. Whether you are the one returning home or the person who stayed home, understanding some of this transition will be helpful.

GOING HOME WELL—BREAKS, SUMMER, AND BEYOND

Almost every college student returns home at some point, whether it is for Christmas break or at the end of the year, or maybe every weekend to do laundry. Going home is normal. Yet not many college students have learned to go home *well*. What does that mean? Does it involve traveling in style—like in a sweet car or with a beautiful person on your arm? No. Going home well means you have been intentional in taking into account the many changes and transitions you have experienced and how the people at your house and in your town have not been on that same journey—at least, not the exact same journey.

This can be as simple and yet as important as realizing that you may have learned a thing or two in your classes that your friends and family may not be familiar with or even never have heard. Is it your role to return home and attempt to blow them out of the water with demonstrations of your great wisdom and academic prowess? That would be an example of going home poorly. And it is important to keep in perspective that, although you have learned "a lot" in your Introduction to Philosophy or Introduction to Biblical Literature course, there is still much, much more to learn.

Part of the process of learning and growing as a human in this world means growing in humility and appreciation for what we do not know as well as a general appreciation for others' points of view and knowledge. That translates into our actions of not trying to demonstrate how smart we are now that we have a semester or two of college under our belts. It can certainly be a temptation, principally when there is a displayed ignorance about a subject we have recently studied. There is nothing wrong with sharing our learning. It is all about the attitude with which we share it. This is never truer than when this sharing or discussion occurs with our parents or other family members. It is at times like these that our maturity and growth are truly tested. Do we callously spout off facts and figures to prove we are right, or do we compassionately seek to share our new discoveries? It is all about the condition of one's heart and the attitude with which such information is spoken. This is extremely important to remember as a newly minted college student.

It has been said that "the more education one receives, the greater focus on less and less until finally one knows a great deal about nothing." This is an amusing saying that is only partially false. You see, as a college student, the typical and very best (in my opinion) approach you can have to learning is to be exposed to a vast array of subjects, from history to science to literature to theology to economics and everything in between. A college that takes this approach is working to prepare its students for *life*, not just a narrow field or technical vocation.

If you should choose to go on in your studies to earn a master's degree, only one of those fields will be studied. For example, perhaps you go on to study theology in hopes of earning a master of divinity. All the other fields that were studied as a college student besides theology (history, science, literature, economics, etc.) will not be part of that master's program. Make no mistake: Those other disciplines will likely come into play in this new endeavor, but they will only be secondary to the primary study of theology. However, as part of your courses, there will also be a focus on the Bible, church history, philosophy, and, of course, theology.

Let's go on to suppose that you complete your studies and earn a master of divinity but have become so enthralled with the subject that you want to continue to study and so go on to apply and are accepted into a PhD program in theology. Well, now your studies become even more focused. Now all other disciplines have been eliminated from your studies. With each successive step up in degree, a narrower focus of topic comes. This is why the saying says there is a "greater focus on less and less."

What is the point of all this? Simply this: After your first semester, first year, or even after graduation, there is a great deal more to learn. Realizing this helps keep in proper perspective what you do and do not know. Although you are much better for the learning that has taken place, you are no expert, and fully grasping this truth will help temper your attitude toward your family and friends.

Going home well is about choosing this level of humility as well as a respect for the experiences of others. Your experience and journey are unique but no better or worse than those of your friends who chose different paths. It is crucial that you respect the paths they have taken and work to see the validity and positive aspects of them.

Frankly, there is so much more we could have discussed in this book about entering college, and some of those things will be briefly touched on in the last section of the book. What I trust you have learned here is that college can be the adventure of a lifetime. It is an experience that will be filled with all the ups and downs of growth and change but an absolute blast to be embraced and fully lived during all four or five or however many years it takes to complete! Have a most excellent first semester, and may God richly bless you as you grow, learn, and experience the joy of entering college.

POSTSCRIPT: LAST-MINUTE ADVICE

In this final section I have included numerous thoughts, pieces of advice, suggestions and other bits that I hope will be helpful to the prospective college student and his or her parent(s). Take them for what they are worth; I trust that they assist you in this process. This section is not necessarily intended to be read beginning to end but as a resource section and assorted suggestions from one who's been there before.

FINANCIAL AID AND MONEY

Fill out the Federal Application for Student Aid (FAFSA, *www.fafsa.ed.gov*) on time and each year. To miss out on this is to shoot yourself in the foot from a financial aid perspective. The FAFSA website will provide all the information you need about this process.

Apply for scholarships—all of them! I ended up with a $2,000 scholarship (which was a lot of money twenty years ago) basically out of nowhere simply because I adopted an attitude that I would fill out as many scholarship applications as I qualified for. This particular one required that I be a member of a credit union that my parents happened to be members of. So I opened an account and filled out the application. Several weeks later I received a letter in the mail of congratulations. My advice is to apply for scholarships of any and all sizes because you never know what might happen! Even though you may need thousands of dollars, don't skip applying for the $500 or $750 scholarships; there is often less competition for these, and even smaller sums add up. I had this same attitude when in graduate school, and because of that, I paid less each semester I was in school, even though tuition increased during that same period of time. Some free scholarship search sites are: *www.fastweb. com*, *www.collegeboard.org*, *www.scholarships.com*, *www.Petersons.com*.

Budget. Plan a reasonable budget (most colleges will supply you with a suggested budget or what, on average, a student can expect in terms of expenses for food, housing, travel, books, fees, and even entertainment. Do your best to spend less than what is estimated. Plan a budget and then stick to it. With a little work and discipline, you can still take a spring break trip—just maybe not one that involves a cruise ship!

Be wary of borrowing too much. I once met a freshman who had borrowed more than $40,000 for his first year of college. Although it was not technically illegal since living expenses are a valid use of student loans, the $15,000 he used to purchase a truck was excessive. If you end up borrowing a bit more than you need, fine, but do not spend it frivolously; you *will* have to pay it back, you know! Instead, keep all of it in a separate account and do not spend it on anything but necessities for college.

Be careful with credit cards. Getting your first credit card during college can be a good idea. It can be a good way to establish credit, and many banks are glad to approve college students' applications. My advice is to not get a card with a higher credit limit than you can pay off in a month—maybe $500 (maybe less!) is about right. And then be sure to pay it off *every* month! Do not ever go over your limit unless in an emergency.

Don't ever go to a Payday Loan or other type of quick-cash store. If you ever find yourself in need of cash, no matter what you do, never go to this type of store. They typically charge a silly amount of interest to utilize their services. In my opinion, these stores ought to be outlawed because they prey on people in desperate need.

Should you work? If you can avoid working more than on a part-time basis, do so. In fact, if you can avoid working at all, especially during your first year, do so. I made the mistake of working too much during my freshman year (one of my many mistakes that year), and it seriously cut down on the time I ought to have been cultivating friendships and getting acquainted with college life. However, many students must work some to afford college. If this is you, look into job opportunities on campus. They may not pay a great deal, but they are convenient, will work around your schedule, and allow you to be gone for holidays and breaks.

PACKING/DORM ROOMS

If there is one thing about this topic I hope you retained from the earlier in this book, it is that you should not wait to pack until the last minute! It is a good idea to begin this process well in advance. Your college will supply you with a list of all that comes in your dorm room as well as suggestions of what else you may want to bring. Lots of websites make suggestions about this as well, so I will not include a list here. It is helpful, for example, to know whether your dorm lounge has a microwave. If it does, you really do not need one in your room (and many universities prohibit them in individual rooms anyway). Keep in mind that dorm rooms are small, so taking as little as possible is an important practice. Another thing to find out is whether the college allows students to store belongings on campus between school years. This is not typical but can sometimes be arranged.

A final thought: Don't skip living in the dorms for your first year. This is a unique college experience and one not to be missed. The social immersion into college life that takes place in the dorms is a terrific introduction to college. Although you may think it is expensive to live in the dorms and purchase a meal plan, the cost of not surrounding yourself in the freshman experience may prove to be even higher. Lifelong friendships are forged in the crucible of dorm life. Don't miss out on this!

CAR OR BIKE?

If you can avoid bringing a car to campus your first year, I would encourage it. Cars on campus can be attractive targets for thieves, they are often borrowed by friends (or at least asked to be borrowed), parking can be an issue, and they are usually an unnecessary expense and headache.

A good bike is often the only needed source of transportation while on campus. Not only is it efficient and parking easy to find, it is a great source of exercise. Get a good, strong lock and use it! Granted, this leaves trips home a bit trickier, but many colleges feature a rides board where you can connect with folks who are headed in your direction during breaks, and for a portion of the cost of gas, you can get home.

HOME

Should you go home on weekends? My suggestion for you is to be involved in the campus community, both during the week and on the weekends. This is particularly important in your first year. By staying around on the weekends, you will invest in friendships with other freshmen and co-eds. This is so important and something students who go home often totally miss. This is not to say you should miss out on an important celebration with your family or an opportunity to take a trip home occasionally; just don't make it a habit. Instead, let your habit be to stay on campus and get to know what college life is like on the weekends on your campus and with your new friends.

FINDING A CHURCH

My strong suggestion is that you find a church early on during your freshman year. Make it a point to visit a series of churches during your first few weeks at school, and then go back to the ones you liked for a second look. A church family can be the source of incredible support and help during your college years. In fact, your church involvement may be the only place you have the privilege to be around children and older adults during the week. Although you may not think you'll miss being around these two groups (particularly if you have younger siblings at home), you may be surprised how insulated you can feel by always being around other twenty-somethings (or teens) in the dorms and at school. That is a crazy aspect of college. Besides the professors and administration, everyone else is basically the same age. However, a church is much more than a diverse group of different ages; it is the body of Christ, and the mystery of that is that, when we are together in the worshiping community of Jesus followers, we both embody and encounter the risen and living God of the universe. Who wants to miss out on that?

If you attend a Christian school, you might find yourself in a situation where you are required to attend a certain number of student chapel services per week or per semester. Though these services can be great opportunities to connect with and contribute to the body of Christ, *do not* let them stand in for off-campus church services. It might seem tedious to attend so many services in one week, but you will benefit more than you realize from having a place to connect to the body of Christ outside your campus. Plus, think about the significant relationships you'll make…and the home-cooked meals you could get…and places to do your laundry for free! Trust me on this.

ATHLETICS

Should you participate in sports? If you have been given a scholarship to play, then this is a moot point. However, if you are thinking about walking on (which means joining a team or sport without any financial obligation), my advice is to first understand what joining entails. I was a walk on for the track and field team my freshman year. What I did not understand clearly was that I was committing to practices five and six days during the week for three to four hours. On top of this, I planned to work (which I didn't really need to do) about fifteen to twenty hours per week as well. This resulted in me essentially signing my life away way too early.

Although I enjoyed the physical training and the relationships, if I could do it all again, I would not join the track team. Frankly, I was not good enough to compete at the collegiate level (especially in Division I). However, the track team took everyone, so I was not cut. A better choice for me would have been to participate in intramurals—a less competitive league where teams on campus compete against other teams on campus—or even a just a club sport team like ultimate Frisbee. These opportunities afford an outlet for the high school athlete (like me) who still wants to compete.

AVOIDING COMMON PITFALLS

Boyfriends/girlfriends. Do not be in a hurry to begin a relationship at college. Learn to be comfortable as a one instead of needing to be a couple. The right relationship will happen in time. Treat yourself and others with respect, and avoid the temptation to hook up (meaning, make out with someone when not in a relationship) with attractive co-eds. Unfortunately, this is a growing reality on college (and even high school) campuses but not a reality that is helpful or uplifting for anyone.

Exclusive friendships. Avoid friends who want you all to themselves. This is not friendship, this is ownership. Be friends with a variety of people. You have nothing to lose by being kind and a friend to everyone.

Isolating relationships. Similar to above. Avoid relationships—especially romantic ones—that require all your attention to be spent on only this one person. Run from these situations!

Don't do too much. I cannot stress this enough. There are so many good things to be involved in at college. Your job is to figure out the few things that are the *best* for you to do and then do them well. Doing too much will only frustrate you and those depending on you because you will not be able to do *anything* well.

Don't fail out! Although college is "10 percent academics and 90 percent everything else," you have *got* to do well with the 10 percent! Don't miss this all-important truth just because there is a great party down the hall—every night! Be disciplined enough to get your studies done earlier in the day so you can socialize in the evenings.

GOOD LUCK

That's enough. I think you have probably got the idea. I sincerely hope the school in which you find yourself today is the same one that is printed on your diploma four or five years from now. Regardless of that, though, enjoy these years. Do all you can to embrace your college experience. Do not simply *get through it*, as if it is like some sort of disease or sickness. Really lean into it. Grab it by the horns and ride it for all it is worth! As much as it is up to you, give yourself completely to living, learning, loving, and laughing during this period of your life. Avoid some of the stupid mistakes I made and make the very most of each day. Blessings to you in your own personal adventure of college!

NOTES

NOTES

NOTES

NOTES

NOTES

NOTES